I Believe God

Book 1

Rev. Dr. Bobby R. Showers, Sr.

Edited by: Claude R. Royston

BK Royston Publishing LLC

Jeffersonville, IN

BK Royston Publishing
P. O. Box 4321
Jeffersonville, IN 47131
502-802-5385
http://bkroystonpublishing.com
bkroystonpublishing@gmail.com

© Copyright – 2010 – Dr. Bobby Showers, Sr.

All Rights Reserved. No part of this book may be reproduced, stored in a retrieval system, or transmitted by any means without the written permission of the author.

Published by: BK Royston Publishing LLC
Cover & Layout by: BK Royston Publishing LLC
Photography: Clicks on Purpose

ISBN-13: 978-0615937144
ISBN-10: 0615937144

Printed in the United States of America

Acknowledgements

First, and foremost I want to thank the Holy Father, by the Son, through the Holy Ghost for saving me and putting me in the ministry. Thanks, be to God for my parents the late Nathaniel L. Showers, Sr. and Arlene M. Showers. My dear mother was saved in the year I was born, 1950.

Special thanks to my extraordinary wife of 40 plus years, our ten talented children who are now national recording artists, along with our three son-in-laws, two daughter-in-laws, 12 grandchildren and 1 great grandchild. To my siblings who have been an inspiration to me, especially Dr. Lavanner Brown who encouraged me to enroll in Seminary School.

To the late Rev. T.J. Johnson, the first preacher I knew and who taught and showed me how to live a Christian life. To my pastor since 1972, Rev. Dr. Samuel C. Brown, Sr., pastor of Mt. Vernon Missionary Baptist Church where I preached my first sermon in 1981 and was ordained by Dr. Brown the following year. To the pastor who baptized me, the late Rev. Versey Smith and his nephew, Rev. Frank Baker of St. Mary Baptist Church in Livingston, Louisiana. Thanks, be to God for my church family who has allowed me to be their pastor: First and foremost, Community Baptist Church of Fluker, Louisiana, where I started in September 1982. Rose Valley Baptist Church, of Roseland, Louisiana, where I have been since March 1988. To Zion Travelers Missionary Baptist Church, of Independence, Louisiana, where I have served as Pastor since August 2011. Special thanks go to Mrs. Sabrina James and Mrs. Lasaundra Pitts for their work and to Mrs. Barbara

Hardesty for her untiring labor.

Rev. Dr. Bobby R. Showers, Sr.

11249 Wardline Rd • Hammond, LA 70401
Phone: (225) 567-5240 • Email:
drbrshowers50@yahoo.com

Objective

As 1 Timothy 4:16 states, I will take heed unto myself and unto the doctrine; continuing in them: for in doing this I shall save myself, and them that hear me. For this reason, I will teach and preach no other doctrine.

PERSONAL

Born To the late Nathaniel L. Showers, Sr. and Arlene M. Showers Family: United in Holy Matrimony with Oralean J. Showers on June 30, 1973, unto this union ten talented children were born. They are known as the Showers Family Gospel Singers, who sing God's praises.

MINISTERIAL EXPERIENCE

Preached Initial Sermon Mt. Vernon Baptist Church, Hammond, LA Dr. Samuel C. Brown, Pastor	April 1981
Ordained to the Ministry Mt. Vernon Baptist Church, Hammond, LA Dr. Samuel C. Brown, Pastor	June 1982

Community Baptist Church   September 1982 – August 2011
   Fluker, LA

Rose Valley Baptist Church   March 1988 - Present
   Roseland, LA

Zion Travelers Missionary Baptist Church August 2011 to Present
   Independence, LA

RELIGIOUS POSITIONS

President, Third District   Present
   Bogue Chitto Baptist Association

Bible Teacher, Third District   Present
   Bogue Chitto Baptist Association
   Sunday School – School Congress Ministers Class

Chairman, Third District   Present
   Bogue Chitto Baptist Association's
   Evangelical Board

First Vice Moderator of the Third District   Present
   Bogue Chitto Baptist Association

Recording Secretary, LA Home & Foreign Mission   Present
   Baptist State Convention, Inc.

Assistant Treasurer of N.B.C.A., Inc., Int'l   Present
    Board Member of Christian Community Network

Recording Secretary, Tangipahoa   Past
    Interdenominational Ministers

Elected Sunday School Missionary   May 1982
    Hammond, LA

Recording Secretary,   Past
    Amite River Progressive Christian Association

Recording Secretary,   Past
    Third District Bogue Chitto Baptist Association

FOUNDATIONS

Founder & Coordinator,   Present
    Annual Community Revival, Roseland, LA

Coordinator of Joint Fellowship (Four Churches)   Present
    Roseland, LA

CIVIC POSITIONS

President of CARE (Churches and Responders Engaged)   Present
Recording Secretary for Home away from home   Present
Board Member on the WIA Board   Present

EDUCATION

Doctor of Theology Degree,   July 1998
    Andersonville Baptist Seminary Camilla, GA

Master of Theology Degree, Andersonville Baptist Seminary Camilla, GA	April 1997
Bachelors of Arts Degree International Bible College Independence, MO	April 1996
Southeastern Louisiana University Hammond, LA	1992-1995
Bible College Degree Lynchburg, VA	May 1990
Broadcasting School Houston, TX	September 1969
West Livingston High School Denham Springs, LA	May 1969

REFERENCE AVAILABLE UPON REQUEST

Introduction

In this ever changing and complex society in which we live right has become wrong, and wrong has become right. Who are we to believe the lawmakers in Washington D.C., our state legislatures, politicians, or will we believe God? What brought about this book, "I Believe God" was the Holy Spirit directing me to do a series of the rightly divided Word of God." It is a sin for anyone to wrongly divide the word. We must follow the Lord's command in II Timothy 2:15.

It is my prayer that after you have read this book you will say with the Apostle Paul, "I Believe God." This whole chapter of Acts is given up to the reality of a shipwreck. Paul, a prisoner in chains, was on his way to Rome, to stand before Caesar. The ship in which he was aboard had reached the Fair Havens, a beautiful port where much time was spent. Paul, at this point admonished Julius the centurion and others, saying "Sirs, I perceive that this voyage will be with hurt and much damage, not only of the cargo and ships, but also of our lives. Nevertheless the centurion believed the master and the owner of the ship, more than those things which were spoken by Paul."

Isn't that like a lot of folks you know both in sacred, as well as secular history who would rather hear others over the preacher? My brothers and sisters, if the preacher is declaring "Thus saith the Lord," you had better hear him, for he is God's man, in God's place, speaking for God. No doubt the centurion said, "This land lubber of a preacher may do pretty well for a pulpit, but he doesn't know a square yard from a crossjack when it comes to a ship." So he gave command to sail on.

Nevertheless, Paul was right and the captain wrong. The text says, "Not long after there arose against the ship a tempestuous wind called Euroclydon, which meant a southeast wind that stirs up waves." The ship was in trouble and the lives of the 276 people that were on board were threatened. "But after long abstinence Paul stood forth in the midst of them, and said, Sirs you should have hearkened unto me, and not have loosed from Crete, and to have gained this harm and loss."

Why would Paul talk to the crew this way? Was he being sarcastic? Not at all; for Paul was not taunting them with an "I told you so," but was reminding them that through the leadership of the Holy Spirit, he had predicted this very problem. In the future, they listened to him and their lives were spared according to verses 30-32 of the text. Paul, seeing and knowing the fretfulness of the centurion and others, gave them some good news from the Lord. He said, "And now I exhort you to be of good cheer: "For there stood by me this night the angel of God, whose I am and whom I serve, saying Fear not, Paul; thou must be brought before Caesar, and lo, God hath given thee all them that sail with thee. "What a man this servant of the most High God was, because the Lord spared all the lives aboard the ship because of Paul. Oh friends, think about how many people's lives are still going on, because the Lord had one of his servants aboard. It ought to behoove every sinner to give his or her life to Christ because the Lord has allowed your golden moments to roll on a few days longer because his child interceded on your behalf.

Paul, here in verse 25, sets forth a bold statement, "Wherefore, sirs, be of good cheer: for I believe God that it shall be even as it was told me." Those three words, "I believe God," are the words every born again believer ought to say twenty-four hours a day, 365 days a year, and 366 of a leap year. Have you ever pondered and wondered why there is so much trouble in Christendom today? It is simply because we don't believe God. The apostle Paul could say, "Nevertheless, I am not ashamed: For I know in whom I have believed, and am persuaded that he is able to keep that which I have committed unto him against that day." (II Timothy 1:12) Oh in this day and hour, for those of us that are believers in Christ, stand up and say as never before, "I believe God." When the homosexuals and lesbians of our day are marrying each other, we ought to tell them, "I believe God." For God said, "If a man also lies with mankind, as he lieth with a woman, both of them have committed an abomination: they shall surely be put to death; their blood shall be upon them." (Leviticus 20:13)

Do you and I believe God about this issue, or the Supreme Court of Massachusetts that made it legal? To make matters worse the United States Supreme Court failed to overturn this ruling, therefore they don't believe God either. Dr. John Rice said, "Never put a question mark where God has put a period." When most Americans think it acceptable to gamble away that which the Lord has graciously blessed them with, I believe God in what he says about the issue. "He that by usury and unjust gain increaseth his substance, he shall gather it for him that will pity the poor." (Proverbs 28:8). "He that maketh haste to be rich shall not be innocent" (Proverbs 28:20)

"For the love of money is the root of all evil which while some coveted after, they have pierced themselves through with many sorrows." (I Timothy 6:10). Thou shalt not covet" (Exodus 20:17).Gambling, as someone wrote, is not acting on faith. It is taking an artificial risk for hope of excessive gain far beyond what the investment of time, money or skill would justify. A gamble is a transaction whereby your gain is someone else's loss. When you gamble, you try to exploit chance; you hope that you will be the only lucky one. So gambling is the opposite of faith. The Bible says, "The just (Christian) should live by faith." (Galatians 3:11b) Will we believe God on this issue or man?

Another hot topic in our society where we ought to say, "I believe God," is the issue of abortion, which is the killing of innocent babies. You and I both know that it should be "The Lord giveth and the Lord taketh away." (Job 1:21)But man believing in self and not God decides who should live and not die. Man says, "It's not a life until full development." But God told Jeremiah, "Before I formed thee in the belly, I knew you." (Jeremiah 1:5) Also at the moment of conception life begins for the child and the Lord has a record of every child that has been conceived. Oh friends today, don't believe the pro-choice advocate which says, "A woman has the right to choose", but believe God when He says, "Lo children are a heritage of the Lord: and the fruit of the womb is his reward." (Psalms 127:3) In this day and hour like never before, let each of us say, "I believe God."

From the Bible, which should be the believer's guide, let each of us say, "I believe God.

"It was God's word that spoke it, He took the bread and broke it and with the word did make it, that I believe and take it." DL Wilmington

Table of Contents

Acknowledgments

Introduction

Chapter 1	Hell The Forgotten Place	1
Chapter 2	Children and Parents, Tattoos, Dress, Alcohol	13
Chapter 3	Women Preachers, Lord's Supper, Pastors and Members	27
Chapter 4	Fathers	41
Chapter 5	Retribution, Dancing	55
Chapter 6	Marriage-Part I	67
Chapter 7	Marriage Part II	81
Chapter 8	Divine Healing	95
Chapter 9	Giving, Secret Orders, Spiritual Renewal	109
Chapter 10	King James Version, Capital Punishment, The Christian Life	125
Chapter 11	Civil Government	139
	Bibliography	153

Chapter 1

Hell: The Forgotten Place

In this modernistic society in which we live many changes have taken place. In 1965 I was given an oration by my high school English Teacher Mrs. Ophelia Atkins. The first paragraph is still in my memory bank which said, "Our society is great, society is changing. Changes are taking place all around us. "I must say that is a true statement about society, but when it comes to Almighty God; He remains "the same yesterday, today and forever more." (Hebrews 13:8). Knowing this we should ever be mindful of the Bible which is the Word of God. In God's word we have various teachings on a number of things, but one doctrine that we in Christendom don't teach or preach anymore is the reality of Hell. We have become so refined today that we no longer believe in a literal Hell. Please don't say, "Yes I do preacher." Well I believe as the late

Oliver B. Greene that if we believe in Hell, why don't we act like it by proclaiming it. One of the greatest evangelist of this country commented on CNN's Larry King live a few years ago that, "We are not sure whether or not there is any literal fire in Hell." I have to wonder what Bible that preacher is preaching from. The Lord Jesus Christ preached more about Hell than He did Heaven. What is Hell? It is the place of eternal punishment for the unrighteous. The King James Version has this word (Hell) to translate Sheol (O.T.) and Hades(N.T.) words used respectively, for the abode of the dead. Hell is also translated Gehenna, the Greek form of the Hebrew phrase that means" the vail of Hinnom a valley west and south of Jerusalem."

In the time of Jesus the valley of Hinnom was used as the garbage dump of Jerusalem. Into it were thrown all the filth and garbage of the city, including the dead bodies of animals and executed criminals. To consume all this, fires burned constantly. Maggots were seen in the filth.

Theologians say "When the wind blew from that direction over the city, an awful stench was quite evident. At night wild dogs howled as they fought over the dead bodies. The Lord Jesus used this awful scene as a symbol of Hell. In essence our Lord said "Do you want to know what Hell is like?" Then look at Gehenna. Hell may be described as God's worldwide garbage dump. All that is unfit for Heaven will be thrown into Hell. How long has it been since you tuned into a religious broadcast, whether on TV or the radio and heard a sermon on Hell. For some reason we have gotten to the place where we either are ashamed or afraid to teach or preach on the subject. Our silence on the matter is sending people to Hell.

Many of us today are educated beyond our intelligence. The Bible says this, "Ever learning, and never able to come to the knowledge of the truth." (2 Timothy 3:7). In essence we are portraying "Ignorance in action." Someone has rightly said, "We've got so many material things in this world that Heaven is no longer attractive to us. " Look around you, we have every comfort there is, so Hell doesn't mean as much as it did to our fore parents. Many of them believed it was a place of fire and brimstone, but mankind as a whole think of Hell as a vacation resort. No one who has ever overdosed on alcohol or drugs has ever beheld anything that can be compared to one second in Hell. No one who has ever been put in a padded cell has experienced even a small portion of Hell. No place, no time, nowhere, no matter how severe or depraved the problem, nothing can be compared to one split second of Hell.

      Dr. Tom Malone once said, "There is no back door in Hell and the only way to get out is to stay out." My dear friends once there, no one can escape. For as the Lord God shut up the ark after Noah and his family entered, so once men and women has been cast into Hell, the Holy Father is through with them. Though Hell may be a forgotten place to the multitudes, the Lord is saying to us today "I have not forgotten about it." The Lord would say, not only have I not forgotten about it, the rich man in our text has not forgotten either. He the rich man could say I found out the split second I died in my sin that Hell is a real place with real people in it. Allow me with the Lord's help to set forth to you some verifiable facts about this place called Hell.

I. Who Made Hell?

Allow me to humbly set forth that it was not the Devil's idea to create it. Who in their right mind would create or make a place for their own doom? Not one. So Hell was not the Devil's idea. This may shock some of us, but in the beginning there was no Hell, for the Bible says, "In the beginning God created the Heaven and the earth" (Genesis 1:1). God only created what was needed, but how long afterward no one knows that the Devil and his angels rebelled against God in Isaiah 14 and Ezekiel 28. After his rebellion the Lord needed a place for them so Hell was made for them. According to St. Matthew 25:41 the Bible says, "Hell was prepared for the Devil and his angels." The Holy Father, by the Son, through the Holy Ghost did not prepare it for mankind, but since man seemingly wants to follow the Devil and his angles in rebellion against Him, the Lord according to Isaiah 5:14 sets forth, "Therefore Hell hath enlarged herself and opened her mouth without measure." So the Lord wants all to know that Hell is the place for all unbelievers who would rather choose the Devil's way over His way. He further says "If you want it like the Devil, his angels and the rich man of the text, it's all yours." The Triune God once again says to each of us,"I am the one who made Hell."

II. What Kind of Place Is Hell?

Before many of us take a vacation we gather as much information as possible about our destination. Well dear friends, allow me to set forth to you the kind of place

Hell is according to God's word. Before I give you the Biblical facts please don't let anyone hoodwink, bamboozle, or deceive you into believing that Hell is not a place of real fire, but only a state of mind. Please brothers and sisters hear these authentic, as well as validated truths about Hell.

    1. Hell is a place where people pray. (Luke16:23)

    2. Hell is a place where they scream for mercy. (Luke 16:24)

    3. Hell is a place where the wicked will be tormented with fire. (Luke 16:24). Torment means to be tortured, distressed, vexed and twisted. The flames will make you twist.

    4. Hell is a place where you are not wanted. (Luke 16:28). Is there anyone here that wants to go to a place they are not wanted? If you die and go to Hell, the first thing you will discover is that God didn't want you there, and second that you're not wanted.

    5. Hell is a place of memory. (Luke 16:25) Those souls that are there now as the rich man of our text, as well as those that will go, memory will be a haunting factor. They will remember the pleas of the preacher to "Come to Jesus as well as the appeal of others."

6. It is also a place for murderers, liars, fearful and the abominable. (Revelation 21:8)

7. A place where their worm does not die (Mark 9:44, 46, 48). Oh the horrors of Hell that the Lord would mention it 3 times in vss. 44, 46 & 48.

8. A place where they have no rest. (Revelation 14:11)

9. A place of outer darkness. (Matthew 8:12)

10. A place of weeping and gnashing of teeth, (Matthew 8:12)

11. A place where they curse God. (Revelation 16:11)

12. A place of everlasting burning. (Isaiah 33:14)

13. A lake of fire into which people are cast alive. (Revelation 19:20)

Theses thirteen things should be enough for anyone in their right mind to say, "Hell is not my kind of place and I am going to give my life to Christ, so I will not go there.
We have heard from God's word concerning: Who made Hell? And what kind of place is Hell? And now let us lastly see where Hell is.

III. Where is Hell?

There is no need any longer for no one to say, "I don't know where Hell is", when the Word of God is clear on the matter. It is down, for Heaven us up. Remember the Apostle Paul who stated in 2 Corinthians 12:2, "How he was caught up to the third Heaven." Also in Acts 1:9 concerning the Lord Jesus after His resurrection and tabernacling here 40 days, the Bible says, "And when He had spoken these things, while they beheld, He was taken up; and a cloud received Him out of their sight." There are other scriptures about Heaven being up, but our focus is again the locality of Hell. Dear friends' Hell is down. In Isaiah 14:9 it says, "Hell from beneath is moved for thee to meet thee at thy coming…" (Isaiah 14:15), yet thou shalt be brought down to Hell to the sides of the pit. Ezekiel 31:16 says, "I made the nations to shake at the sound of his fall, when I cast him down to Hell with them that descend into the pit." Ezekiel 31:17says, "They also went down into Hell with him unto them that be slain with the sword." Also Ezekiel 32:27.

Lastly to illustrate from the word of the Lord that Hell is down the Bible records in Numbers 16 about Korah, Dathan, Abriam, and On who withstood Moses along with 250 princes. These men had the audacity as some today who think they are on par with God's man. My friends Korah and his gang found out that you don't mess with the chosen of the Lord. The Bible records because of their rebelliousness, "The Lord God caused the earth to open up and Korah with all of them went down alive into the pit and the earth closed upon them, and they perished from among the congregation."

Conclusion:

O friends, Hell and Heaven are calling your name. Who will you listen to and follow? Hell where the Devil, his angels and all unbelievers will be and awaits those who remain in their sin. But the Heaven, the Lord Jesus Christ's place is calling and saying, "Don't go to Hell, but come unto me, all you that labour and are heavy laden and I will give you rest." (Matthew 11:28).

CHAPTER 2

Children, Parents, Tattoos Dress and Alcohol

In part one of our message on I believe God, the Lord enabled us to see the Apostle Paul sailing on the Mediterranean Sea to make his appeal before Caesar. Paul had warned Julius the centurion when they reached the Fair Havens, "Sirs, I perceive that this voyage will be with hurt and much damage, not only of the cargo and ships, but of our lives."

As it was then, so is it now that the centurion believed the master and owner of the ship, more than those things which were spoken by Paul. No wonder the Bible says "There is nothing new under the sun." (Eccl. 1:9b) As Julius did not believe God's anointed, so are there many who still do not believe the words God gives the preacher today. When they did not believe the apostle, a tempestuous wind called Euroclydon came up which threatened the lives of all 276 that were aboard the ship. The text says, "But after long abstinence (or of not saying anything) Paul stood and said, "Sirs you should have listened to me."

And now I exhort you to be of good cheer: for there shall be no loss of any man's life among you, but of the ship. For there stood by me this night the angel of God, whose I am, and whom I serve, saying, "Fear not Paul; thou must be brought before Caesar; and lo God hath given thee all them that sail with thee."Notice verse 25 of which our focus will be "Wherefore, sirs, be of good cheer; for I believe God that it shall be even as it was told me." How many of us can emphatically say "I believe God?" To believe God is to say, "I believe his word." If you and I don't believe God's word, we certainly can't believe God. For us to believe means we accept what he says from Genesis 1:1 to Revelation 22:21.

Who did Paul believe again and in whom do we believe? Paul could say, "I know in whom I believe and I am persuaded that he is able to keep that which I have committed unto him against that day." (II Tim. 1:12) In I believe God part one on last Sunday, I said I believe God on the homosexual and lesbian issue that "If a man also lie with mankind, as he lieth with a woman both of them have committed an abomination." (Leviticus 20:13) The same is true with a woman lying with another woman.

I believe God on the gambling issue Proverbs 28:8; 28:20; I Tim. 6:10; Exodus 20:17. Gambling is exploiting chance; you hope that you will be the only lucky one. Gambling is the opposite of faith. "The just (Christian) should live by faith." (Galatians 3:11b) Also I believe God on the Abortion Issue. On this great day I also believe God about other things, namely (1) Children and their Parents, (2) Markings or Tattoos, (3) How we should dress, (4) Alcohol.

I. Children and Their Parents

We can't believe what society says about children and their parents. Society says put the children in time out as their manner of discipline, but the Lord says "Withhold not correction from the child; for if thou beatest him with the rod, he shall not die." (Proverbs 20:30). Parents, we must believe God in the disciplining of our children and no one else. Parents, you all must be together in this matter of discipline. One can't want it and the other not want to do it. For if the children can detect division between us on the matter; it will make things worse. There must be agreement on what is to be done and hold fast to it.

The breakdown in society of our young people cannot be contributed to the schools, the church, or law enforcement. The failure is in our homes. Our children were not born in school, in the church, nor in jail, but in

our homes. If the parents don't care about their children's welfare, the evidence will come forth in them. Parents, we have a divine responsibility to "Train up our children in the way of the Lord…" (Proverbs 22:6) and "To bring them up in the nurture and admonition of the Lord." (Ephesians 6: 4) Children, you also have a divine responsibility as set forth by the Bible. "Children obey your parent in the Lord; for this is right. Honor thy father and thy mother (Which is the first commandment with promise) that it may be well with thee, and that thou mayest live long on the earth." (Ephesians 6:1-3). The children will say, what will be the consequences preacher if I don't obey them? Let the Bible answer that for you. "Be not over much wicked, neither be thou foolish: why shouldest thou die before thy time." (Ecclesiastes 7: 17).
A lot of young folks are in the graveyard today because Mama and Daddy could not tell them anything. They

thought as a lot of our youth are still thinking; that we are trying to hold them back from having fun with their friends.

Hear me young people and hear me well. If your friends are not about what is right, you stay away from them as you would a rattlesnake. We have been where you are trying to get to, and can tell you about the pot holes of life. Obey your parents because one day you will be one, and if you have disobeyed your parents, your children will disobey you.

II. Tattoos and Marks

I know in this day that tattoos have become a popular thing with many of our young people, as well as others. The question remains, "Will you believe God or others?" The Lord says in Leviticus 19:28, "Ye shall not make any cutting in your flesh for the dead, nor print any marks upon you: I am the Lord." The tattoo is a permanent mark or design fixed upon the body by a process of pricking the skin and inserting an indelible color under the skin. Why would folks mess up what God has beautified? The Lord gave you that body the way he wanted it and if we can't enhance it God's way, we ought to leave the tattooing of it alone. I have never seen a beautiful tattoo.

I know many of our athletes have them, but that doesn't make it right. I see young ladies and young men with them on their legs, arms, and other body parts which is disgraceful. If you want a mark, tell the Lord to give you the permanency of His Holy Spirit. When others try and entice you to get tattooed, tell them the Lord has already done it by His Spirit.

III. How We Should Dress

Should a Christian wear anything? No. You and I both know that the world has its standards for dressing, but we as children of God also have standards. A woman should not look like a man in her dressing, neither shall a man look like a woman in his. Some things are moral, whereas, others are immoral. The Bible says, "The woman's hair is her glory," (I Cor. 11:15), but in my years I have seen men make it theirs. The Bible says, "The woman is the glory of the man, (I Cor. 11:7) not his hair."

I have known men to spend more on their hair than women. Back in the late seventies I can never forget a brother which said, "Don't my hair look better than hers." What a shame. Mothers and fathers, if you have a son let him be a son, and not make him a daughter by plaiting his hair. The responsibility of that child is in your hands. I don't care how pretty it is, have him to know that the barber is for men and the cosmetologist or beautician is for women.

As for men and women's dress, it should be the kind that brings honor and glory to God. In the Old Testament it was the Lord's concern, as well as the

New Testament. There are two kinds of laws in the Bible, one being ceremonial, with the other being moral. Brothers and sisters, our dress should be of the moral variety. To be moral pertains to the principles of right and wrong. Ladies, it is not moral for you to wear clothing that reveals some body parts. The same is true with you, brothers. Morally, if a dress or pants are too tight and too short it becomes enticing, and brothers, for you to wear pants or shorts that reveal your underwear that is not moral. Brothers and sisters, don't use your dressing outwardly to try and win over the opposite sex, but have a dressed up heart and soul to draw a man or woman. The Bible says, "Who's adorning, let it not be that outward adorning of plaiting (braiding) the hair, and of wearing of gold or of putting on of apparel, but let it be the hidden man of the heart in that which is not corruptible, even the ornament of a meek and quiet spirit, which is in the sight of God of great price." (I Peter 3:3-4).

IV. The Matter of Alcohol

Yes brothers and sisters, alcohol. It has been said that, "Alcohol is America's most costly luxury." Alcohol has ruined multitudes of men, women, boys, and girls who have been deceived into partaking of it. You have heard this commercial "When you say Bud, you have said it all." That is: you must drink it, because no other drink can do what it can. Friends, the only thing that can bring you all is a drink of the Holy Spirit not Budweiser beer.

Much has been said by those who try and justify drinking alcohol. One of the main things that is said, "Jesus drank wine." He sure did, but not the kind that men say he did. There are two words for wine in the Bible, one is "Tirosh" is the unfermented kind. The other is "Yayin" is fermented. Yayin wine is the one that causes all the trouble and the one that the Bible speaks against. "Wine is a mocker, strong drink is raging, and whosoever is deceived thereby is not wise." (Proverbs 20:1).

"Who hath woe? Who hath sorrow? Who hath contentions? Who hath babbling? Who hath wounds without cause? Who hath redness of eyes? They that tarry long at the yayin (wine); they that go to seek mixed wine. Look not upon the wine (yayin) when it is red, when it giveth its color in the cup, when it moveth itself aright. At the last it biteth like a serpent, and stingeth like an adder (snake)."

"Thine eyes shall behold strange women, and thine heart shall utter perverse (corrupt) things." (Proverbs 23:29-33). That's what yayin will do for you. Yayin (wine) causes the brain cells to die when it enters the blood stream. It also affects the heart, liver and kidneys. Also, concerning yayin wine, the Lord says,

"But they also have erred through wine, and through strong drink are out of the way. The priest and the prophet have erred through strong drink; they are swallowed up of wine, they are out of the way through strong drink, they err in vision, they stumble in judgment." (Isaiah 28:7).

In Joel 1:5, the Lord says, "Awake ye drunkards and weep; and wail, all ye drinkers of wine, because of the new wine; for it is cut off from your mouth." In I Corinthians 6:9-10 the Lord gives a list of those who will not enter the kingdom of God and drunkards or those who partake of the yayin will not enter. Then my friends, the Lord warns those who give it to others, "Woe unto him that giveth his neighbor to drink that putteth the bottle to him, and maketh him drunk also, that thou mayest look on their nakedness." (Habakkuk 2:15)

It was yayin wine that caused Noah to get drunk after the flood as recorded in Genesis 9:20-21. It was Yayin wine that caused Lot to commit incest with his own daughters in Genesis 19:30-38. The Tirosh or unfermented wine is what Jesus and His disciples partook of at the Last Supper. It was Tirosh that our Lord was involved with at the wedding in Cana of Galilee.

Conclusion:

How many of us can say like Paul today, "I believe God." For you and I to say it and practice it, is to say, "Lord you have said it and I'm going to stand on it. Lord you went to great lengths to get us this word, and no matter what others say and do, I'm going to believe it." Lord, you gave us the word (Jesus Christ) who came into the world to die on the cross, to be buried, resurrected, go back to the Father, and one day come back and receive us unto Himself that where he is, we will be there also.

CHAPTER 3

Women Preachers, Lord's Supper, Pastors and Members

Again we find the Apostle Paul on the Mediterranean Sea sailing with 275 passengers. This man Paul is on his way to Rome for an appeal before Caesar of which he requested through divine intervention. We all know from the two previous messages that Paul had warned the centurion, Julius, that the voyage to Rome would be with hurt and much damage of the cargo, the ship, and our lives. Disregarding the warning of Paul they sailed any way to their regret a great storm came upon them. Seeing this, the man, of God, after holding his peace for a long time said, "You should have hearkened unto me though you did not." "There is no need to fear, for the angel of God, <u>whose I am,</u> and <u>whom I serve</u> hath assured me that God hath given thee all them that sail with thee." (Acts 27:24)

"Wherefore, sirs, be of good cheer; for I believe God that it shall be even as it was told me." As I said in part one and in part two of this message, can I get you to say with me? "I believe God." Please don't perjure yourself by saying so. Our Heavenly Father like never before needs those of us who say we are Christians to believe him and no one else, for we can't be as Israel was after the death of Joshua. The Bible says, "In those days there was no king in Israel, every man did that which was right in his own eyes." (Judges21:12). Friends, that is pretty much the state we are in now and the Lord is saying, "Church of the Living God awake out of your sleep and believe me."

In our last two messages on "I believe God," we focused on the homosexual and lesbian issue, gambling, Hell, alcohol, tattoos, children and their parents, and how we (the church) should dress. Brothers and sisters, who hear us this day, allow me here in part three of this series, "I believe God" to share with you some other vital issues that we face in this day. (1) Women preachers, (2) The Lord's Supper, and (3) The pastor and members relationship.

I. Women Preachers

Believers in Christ, I believe God on this argument of whether or not women should preach, or call themselves a pastor, elder, evangelist, prophet, apostle or bishop. I have heard and so have you that if they say God called them, that's between them and God. What some are saying is, That's my sister, mother, grandmother, or aunt and I don't believe they would lie. Let us examine the Bible and see who are you going to believe? The women of our day, or God.

"There he goes again" some sister will say, but it's not me it is Him (Lord). I told you he didn't like women. No, it's not I that I don't like you, for I am your friend. "Am I therefore become your enemy because I tell you the truth?" Galatians 4:16. The ones who actually lie to you are the ones that say, "If God could make a mule talk and a rooster to crow; I know he can use a woman to preach." Hear me and hear me well, that mule was a male donkey and the rooster is an adult male of the domestic fowl. So that won't stand up.

Some say and quote Acts 2:17-18, "And it shall come to pass in the last days, saith God, I will pour out my spirit upon all flesh; and your sons and your daughters shall prophesy, and your old men shall dream dreams; and on my servants and on my handmaidens I will pour out my spirit, and they shall prophesy." These verses, brothers and sisters have to do with salvation, not a call to preach.

Still others will utter, "In Christ there is neither male, nor female." That is true but that verse of scripture is also dealing with salvation. Hear what the text says, "For as many of you as have been baptized into Christ have put on Christ. There is neither Jew nor Greek, there is neither bond nor free, there is neither male nor female: for ye are all one in Christ Jesus." (Galatians 3:27-28).

Though men and women quote scripture to try and justify women preachers, the fact remains, "Will you believe God or man?" You can quote any scripture to try and make right what you want to be right, but have you rightly divided the Word of God. It is a sin to wrongly divide the word, especially when we are trying to make what is wrong to be right. How can any man or woman refute, I Timothy 2: 11-12? "Let the woman learn in silence with all subjection. But I suffer not a woman to teach, not to usurp authority over the man, but to be in silence." That verse is as clear as the noon day sun and to refute it is to say, "The moon shines at high noon and the sun gives its light in the night."

When the Lord says, "I suffer not a woman to teach", He does not mean that women should not speak to other women, or children, but that it is against God for a woman to teach or pastor a man. If you and I believe God we will clearly see that women cannot pastor. The Bible says, "This is a true saying, If a man desire the office of a bishop, he (not she) desireth a good work." (I Timothy 3:1)

A bishop then must be blameless, the husband of one wife, vigilant, sober, of good behavior, given to hospitality, apt to teach." (I Timothy 3:2). There are eleven gender specific references in I Timothy 3:1-7 which refute the idea of women serving as pastor. There are times when the Lord speaks inclusively of man and woman, and at other times as in this case, He speaks exclusively to the man. The word bishop is in the masculine and therefore requires a male adult. The husband of one wife also sets forth the same, a male adult.

What about Deborah, Miriam, Anna, and Philip's four daughters. Deborah was a judge in Israel, not a teacher or preacher in the New Testament Church. Anna, Miriam, and Philip's daughters were prophetesses who I'm sure told others about Christ, but not in a place of authority over the man.

In a publication by Pastor Wayne Camp of Pilgrim's Hope B. C. in Memphis, Tennessee entitled, "Should Women Preach", he speaks about Martha Phillips, a Southern Baptist Clergywoman. At the Mt. Vernon B. C. in Arlington, Virginia, where she was serving as interim pastor, she demonstrated her open disobedience to the Word of God by saying, "I don't want to be a youth minister or a music minister. I want to lead a congregation. I <u>think</u> I've been called by God. I don't see how they

(Southern Baptist Convention) can say because you're a woman, you can't be. No she can't be and no other woman can, because it's against God and His word. In fact the convention voted to ban female pastors on June 15, 2000.

Sisters, if you believe God, there will be no way of you doing what the Lord has explicitly said, no matter what your feelings are, or what someone else has said. My dear sisters, don't let the Devil fool you into not believing God, nor the flesh or world. I believe God and what He says about women preachers.

II. The Lord's Supper

It is not my supper, nor is it yours, but the Lord's. That is, brothers and sisters, that we should commemorate it as our Lord did. We should not partake of it any kind of way.

When we come to this moment there should be no talking, but meditation and thanksgiving for that glorious night over two thousand years ago. Our mindset for The Lord's Supper ought to be one of reverence and fear to our Lord Jesus Christ.

For if it is not like this we are despising the one who made it possible for us to partake of it. This question comes to mind. "Who should partake of the Lord's Supper?" Anybody, not at all friends for it is only for believers in Christ. It is not to be given to little children who have not confessed Christ and been baptized. You and I that are believers also should not partake of it if we have any ought against our brother or sister, or any known sin, lying or adultery, in our lives. For us to partake of it in such a manner would bring the judgment of God upon us.

The Bible says, "Wherefore whosoever shall eat this bread and drink this cup of the Lord unworthily shall be guilty of the body and blood of the Lord. But let a man examine himself, and so let him eat of that bread and drink of that cup. For he that eateth and drinketh unworthy, eateth and drinketh damnation to himself, not discerning the Lord's body. For this cause many are weak and sickly among you, and many sleep (dead)." (I Cor. 11:27-30).

Oh friends, let us not take the Lord's Supper lightly, but reverently and discreetly, realizing its importance to our Lord. Each of us at this moment ought to see the bread as His broken body and the cup as His blood. We should remind ourselves when we come together that we ought to look backward, inwardly, and forward. We look backward at the awful price our Lord paid on Calvary for our sins. We look inwardly in examining ourselves for participation in it. Lastly, we look forward to the day in which we will drink it new with him in the Father's Kingdom.

We must believe God in what He says about the Lord's Supper. If ever there was a time in our lives when we ought to be at our best behavior, it ought to be when we come to this glorious moment. I can only think of our Lord being in that upper room knowing that Judas would betray him, but yet he went on with the business at hand. That should teach us that when the Lord has something for us to do; we should let nothing deter us from it.

III. The Pastor's and Member's Relationship

The church of the Living God was born on the Day of Pentecost and the Apostle Peter as we know stood to preach a message whereby 3,000 souls were saved. From that day on, the Lord used Peter and the other apostles to proclaim the gospel that men and women might be saved. The Apostle Paul as we know went on three missionary journeys to establish churches and each of them had pastors who were appointed by the Holy Ghost to lead and feed those who had come to Christ.

As these new found churches began their work for the Lord, it was imperative that they knew there had to be a relationship between the pastors and members. The Lord then and now still expects both to fulfill their divine responsibilities toward him and each other. The pastor is expected to take heed unto himself and to the doctrine that the Lord hath given him according to I Timothy 4:16

As a pastor I believe God on this fact of taking heed unto myself. That is I must live a life before God and you all that will bring honor and not dishonor to our Lord. "The way I teach is very important, what I teach is even more important, but how I live is most important."

Also in the pastor and member's relationship, the pastor is to feed God's people with the Word of God. The Bible says, "Feed the flock over which the Holy Ghost hath made you to be overseers." (Acts 20:28)

The Lord through Peter said, "Feed the flock which is among you, taking the oversight thereof, not by constraint, but willingly; not for filthy lucre, but of a ready mind. " (I Peter 5:2). In this day and hour there is a lot of feeding, but not the kind the Lord is calling for. We are not to feed you junk food, but a wholesome meal.

Members, in your relationship with the pastor, the Lord God is expecting you and also commands you to "Obey them that have the rule over you, and submit yourselves: for they watch for your souls, as they that must give account, that they may do it with joy, and not with grief: for that is unprofitable for you." (Hebrews 13:17)

Plain and simple brothers and sisters, the Lord compels you to follow the leadership of your pastor. As members, you are to also take care of your pastor. The Bible says, "Thou shalt not muzzle the ox that treadeth out the corn. And the laborer is worthy of his reward." (I Timothy 5:18) Our Lord also says, "Let the elders that rule well be counted worthy of double honor, especially they who labor in the word and doctrine." (I Timothy 5:17)

The words" double honor", in their original simplicity, mean the pastor is due double pay. Another text of scripture that deals with the pastor's care is I Corinthians 9:7-18, especially I Corinthians. 9:14, which says, "Even so hath the Lord ordained that they which preach the gospel should live of the gospel."
The Bible gives example after example of those who cared for the preacher and how the Lord blessed them. I Kings 17:8-24; II Kings 4:8-10; St Luke 8:2-3.

Conclusion:

Let each of us believe God about women preachers, The Lord's Supper, and the pastor's and members relationship

CHAPTER 4

Father's Responsibility

These words that are spoken here by one of the greatest Christians of all time should serve notice to us that we are to be as he was. This man, Paul, as we know was in the midst of a storm but could say emphatically, "I believe God."

What a testimony to have in the midst of adversity. Knowing and seeing the danger that the ship and all that were aboard found themselves in, these words, "I believe God should be the motto of every born again believer in Christ." I say this because we can't do the right kind of business that ought to be done for the Lord, if we can't believe him. For us to believe God means that we are to trust him in the good times, as well as the bad. The time will come, if it has not when each of us will face a crisis in our lives. What will we do about it? Will we believe God or the opposition? Each of us should thunder out to the Devil, the flesh, and the world, "I believe God." I'm sure there was an uproar on that ship with Paul and the other 275 passengers, who saw nothing but death.

Paul could undoubtedly say, "That's what you all may see, but I see Jesus who has the power over life and death." Brothers and sisters, can we voice the same sentiment as this man of God? If so, we are saying unequivocally, "I believe God."

In our previous messages in this series, "I believe God", we have set forth that to believe God we must accept what his word is saying. Again, I believe God on the homosexual and lesbian issue, gambling, Hell, tattoos, how we should dress, alcohol, women preachers, the Lord's Supper, and the pastor's and member's relationship.

Today, with the Lord's help, let us zero in on "Fathers And Their Responsibility."

Brothers, do we believe God? If we do, the Lord that has made us fathers is calling us, as well as demanding us, to awaken to our divine responsibility. I'm afraid today that many of us as men are shirking our responsibility by shifting the blame elsewhere.

Many a man, instead of taking care of the children whom the Lord has given him, is allowing the women to do what God told us to do. The Lord did not tell the woman to work by the sweat of her face, but he did command the man to do so, according to Genesis. 3:19.

The Lord did not tell the state of Louisiana, nor the government to care for our children, but for us to do so. How despicable it is for a man to be placed on child support because he will not take care of his own children. They did not ask to come here, but you in a moment of pleasure and satisfaction, planted the little Suzie or Jimmy now it's time for you to step up to the plate and care for them.

How sad it is, for a man to go to jail, for not providing for his own child. This past week I saw on the news how many were arrested for child support. Not to mention the millions of dollars this state and other states are spending to care for children who have dead beat dads. I know of a brother who has been running from his divine responsibility for about ten years or more.

Men, why can't we be fathers like Joshua who stated boldly to the tribes gathered at Shechem? "And if it seem evil unto you to serve the Lord, choose you this day whom ye will serve, whether the gods that your fathers served on the other side of the flood, or the gods of the Amorites in whose land ye dwell: But as for me and my house, we will serve the Lord." (Joshua 24:15) Not we will go to Disney Land, to the ball game, or a movie, which is fine, but be sure the Lord is first.

Fathers, when will we take our God ordained place and get about the business he would have us to? I'm afraid today that men are as scarce as they were in Biblical times. Only one Abraham was called out of Ur of Chaldees, only Noah and his three sons were saved from the flood, not to mention Lot being the only man saved out of Sodom and Gomorrah. The Lord told Jeremiah, "Run ye to and fro through the streets of Jerusalem, and see now, and know, and seek in the broad places thereof, if ye can find a man, if there be any that executeth judgment, that seeketh the truth, and I will pardon it." (Jeremiah 5:1).

The Lord, through the prophet Ezekiel, said, "And I sought for a man among them that should make up the hedge, and stand in the gap before me for the land, that I should not destroy it: but I found none." (Ezekiel 22:30). Another thing to us as fathers, and we brothers will do well to take heed: "And ye fathers, provoke not your children to wrath, but bring them up in the nurture and admonition of the Lord." (Ephesians 6:4)

That is, brothers that we must have the patience to raise our children in a loving, Christ honoring manner. Because we get frustrated, we should not take it out on our children. Instead, we should act in love, treating our children as Jesus treats those whom he loves. Brothers, this is vital to our children's development and if we are the right fathers, we will give them a concept of the Lord. J. Wilbur Chapman said, "Every father should be his boy's greatest admiration, and if he lives according to the teaching of God's word, he would start his boy along the way of life with an upward tendency."

I have said it and will say it again that, "I want my daughters to find a husband as good, or better than their dad". Brothers, if you mean right by the Lord, you ought to say the same thing. For in doing so you are taking on a father's responsibility. Brothers, let us not be as the father in the commercial that caught his son smoking and asked,

"Son where did you get that from?" The son hesitantly said, "you dad."

Fathers this day, don't sit there with your chest poked out and say, "I know I'm a man." But the question is, "Who else knows it but you?" Can the Lord say of you and me as he did Abraham? "For I know him, that he will command his children and his household after him." (Genesis 18:19). The Lord in essence was saying," I have confidence in Abraham that he will follow my will for his life and in doing so he will teach his children to do likewise." Abraham my dear brothers allowed God to choose for him. You remember when there was a rift or disagreement between Abraham's herdsmen and his nephew, Lot's herdsmen that Abraham said, "Let there be no strife I pray thee between me and thee, and my herdsmen and thine; for we be brethren."

"Is not the whole land before thee? Separate thyself, I pray thee from me: If thou wilt take the left hand, then I will go to the right, or if thou depart to the right hand, then I will go to the left." (Genesis 13:8-10). We all know that Lot chose the plain of Jordan, that it was well watered everywhere. It was here that Lot got in trouble at Sodom and Gomorrah. But notice Abraham brothers, the Bible says, God spoke to him, "Lift up now thine eyes, and look from the place where thou art northward, and southward, and eastward, and westward: For all the land which thou seest, to thee will I give it, and to thy seed forever. And I will make thy seed as the dust of the earth: so that if a man can number the dust of the earth, then shall thy seed also be numbered." (Genesis 13:14-16)

God can always trust the man who allows him to choose for him the way in which he is to go, the friends with whom he is to have fellowship with. Dad, you are to be your son's role model not Michael Jordan, Kobe Bryant, Cash Money or Fifty Cents. If our sons don't follow our example, let it not be because we were bad ones, but good ones. Though much ado is of good mothers of which I agree, but the Lord has had some good fathers and still does today. Some of you sisters might be saying, "Preacher where are they?"

My life was influenced by a great man of God who died in 1978; and how I thank God all the time for the preacher who didn't just teach me, but lived the life that brought the Lord glory and honor. Brothers what are you and I living for? Are you living for someone to say, "Man he wears some bad rags, he rides in a beautiful automobile, or he lives in a very nice crib?" That may be fine and dandy brothers, but what you and I should be living for is to glorify God in living a Christian life. The position of a father is solemn indeed. Many of us do not appreciate what it means to be the head of a household. It is said a dying mother charged her husband, the father of her children. She said, and I quote, "Bring all these children home with you, and I shall meet you on the other side."

Fathers, be sure to attend Sunday school and Bible class to be taught, so you can teach your children. It is a sad thing that, when crises or the hour of need come in a child's life that too many fathers are not able to speak the word to them in due season. Fathers, let us equip ourselves to give our children the Godly advice they truly deserve. Let us tell them of the three essentials to growth as a father did to his son as he was leaving home. (1) Proper associations, (2) Proper food, (3) Proper exercise.

1. Proper Association

    A. Keep in the light. (I John 1:7) "But if we walk in the light, as he is in the light, we have fellowship one with another, and the blood of Jesus Christ his Son cleanseth us from all sin."

    B. Walk with the wise. (Prov. 13:20) "He that walketh with wise men shall be wise: but a companion of fools shall be destroyed.

    C. Stand aloof from worldly conformity.

    D. Go only where the Spirit leads you. (Romans 8:9-14)

2. Proper Food – I Peter 2:1-3

    A. Have a good reference Bible

    B. Set apart one hour, daily, sacred to Bible Study

    C. Study with a heart prepared for it (Ezra 7-10)

    D. Ask the author of the Book to guide you (Psalm 119:18; John 16:13-14)

    E. Study for personal profit (I Peter 1:22-23; Acts 20:32)

    F. Study to be equipped for service (II Timothy 3:16-17; Ephesians 1:17

    G. Believe promises, heed warnings, obey directions.

    H. Remember it is God's message to you.

3. Proper Exercise – John 13:17

    A. Confess Christ before men (Matt. 10: 32-38)

B. Get into the visible church (Acts 2:42-47; Heb. 10:24-25)

C. Observe the ordinances (Acts 2:38-42; Luke 22:19)

D. Pray daily with your family for God's work (Luke 11: 9-13)

E. Obey every word of Christ (John 2:5; 14:23; 15:7)

F. Use all your time and talents faithfully. "Redeeming the time because the days are evil" (Ephesians 5:16)

G. Give systematically as God has prospered you. "Honor the Lord with thy substance, and with the first fruits of all thine increase. So shall thy barn be filled with plenty, and thy presses shall burst out with new wine." (Proverbs 3:9-10)

Conclusion:

Oh fathers today, I believe God on the responsibility we should have toward our wives, children, and the church of the living God.

Wouldn't Our Church Be Better

If all the sleeping fathers would wake up

If all the lukewarm fathers would get fired up

If all the dishonest fathers would confess up

If all the disgruntled fathers would sweeten up

If all the depressed fathers would look up

If all the mad fathers would make up

If all the gossiping fathers would shut up

If all the dry bone fathers would shake up

If all the bashful fathers would speak up

If all the slothful fathers would speed up

If all the head fathers would charge up

If all the backsliding fathers would straighten up

If all the financially behind fathers would pay up

If all the fathers would show up

If all the faithful fathers would keep up

Then we'll be able to pray up and keep up

Author Unknown

CHAPTER 5

Retribution, Dancing

The Lord God has been with us in our past four messages on, "I Believe God." In those directives we have shown you from God's word what he expects out of us as believers. The Lord has no standard of living for the world, but He does have one for us. All the Lord primarily wants out of those of the world is to "Confess Him with their mouths and believe in Him in their hearts, that God hath raised Jesus from the dead, so they can be saved." (Romans 10:9)

After the Lord has saved men and women from the world, He expects them to believe the Bible which records the words He has spoken. Our Heavenly Father would not have gone to great lengths to give us His word, if He didn't expect us to believe it. Not one child of God can be what he or she ought to be without believing God. The Apostle

Paul of our text wanted the centurion and all that sailed with him on the Mediterranean Sea to know that, "I Believe God." What did he believe about God? He believed that God would do what He said He would do.

The Lord had told Paul, "For there shall be no loss of any man's life among you, but of the ship." This great servant of God did not ponder or wonder whether God would change his mind but said emphatically, "I Believe God." I said on the other Sunday if the Lord takes me, I want those whom I have pastored to say, "He Believed God." I have told you in the previous four messages that I believe God on a number of vital issues. Those things included are gambling, homosexuality and lesbianism, women preachers, tattoos, alcohol, etc.

In our continued series on, "I Believe God," allow me to set forth what I believe about (1) God's law of Retribution and (2) Dancing.

I. There is one thing that the Lord has always wanted mankind to know: there will be a payday for the right and wrong that we do. The Lord has been as clear about everything from Genesis 1:1 to Revelation 22:21. From the beginning He made it clear to Adam when He said, "Of every tree of the garden thou mayest eat: But of the tree of knowledge of good and evil, thou shalt not eat of it: for in the day that thou eatest thereof thou shalt surely die." (Genesis 2:17-18)

Adam evidently thought the Lord was lying and there would be no retribution for what he did, but as soon as he did what God commanded him not do, he found out there were consequences for his actions. Friends, the same holds true for each of us. Never think that God loves you so much that He will not see to you and me reaping what we have sown. David, as the Bible records, was the apple of God's eye, but God's law of retribution caught up with him and he paid dearly for his sin. It was not two acts of adultery, but one that made David weep and howl. That one act caused the death of his baby, the incest of Amnon his son with Tamar his sister, Amnon being killed by Absalom his brother, Absalom's rebellion against his father, and finally the death of Absalom.

God's law of retribution has been at work in each of our lives. Some things that I did before conversion that brought hurt to others came back and brought hurt to me. The Bible says, concerning God's law of retribution, "For they (you and me) have sown the wind, and we shall reap the whirlwind." (Hosea 8:7) In our pleasure we sow our cool breeze, but in our reaping the Lord sends a hurricane or typhoon. No one is exonerated from God's law of retribution.

You may be wrapped up, tied up, and tangled up in the Lord, but one thing I can guarantee you of and that is pay day awaits everyone. Saints, sinners, blacks and whites, the rich as well as the poor. The Lord's clock ticks slow, but believe me it keeps on ticking without electricity or batteries. If everyone could and would believe God on this issue of retribution, our homes, schools, churches, and society would be better.

If men and women who involve themselves in extra marital affairs only knew of the repercussions, they would not do it. If you young folks only knew that sex before marriage is going to bring you heartache you would not do it. If homosexuals and lesbians only knew the recompense for their actions, they wouldn't do it.

If you children that are disobedient to your parents only knew of the consequences you would face, it would awaken you to be obedient. Three things await you for your not obeying: (1) A short life on earth, (2) Your own children disobeying you and (3) The judgment before God.

We that are preachers must also be mindful of God's law of retribution. If we fail to live right, teach, and preach right, the Lord's wrath will be upon us. Not one of us wants to face God and hear him say, "Depart from me, for you had it your way, now it is my way." The drug dealers and those involved in alcohol as well as gambling have a price to pay and will not escape God's law of retribution.

The Bible is plain when it says, "Be not deceived, God is not mocked, for whatsoever a man soweth, that shall he also reap." (Galatians 6:7) If each of us would lie down at night with that verse, awake every morning with it and mediate on it during the day, we would be the kind of vessels ready for the Master's use.

Young people, middle aged, and those up in the years, remember this every time someone tries to get you to do that which is ungodly. Say to them, "I don't want to reap for that." Let each us have the mindset to sow righteous acts, that we can reap the same. God's law of retribution not only applies to the wrong things we do, but also to the right. If you give God his tithes and offerings you will reap having the windows of Heaven open up to pour out blessings that you won't have room enough to receive.

The Lord has many great things for those of us who will live our lives in dedication to Him. Let us, brothers and sisters, receive God's blessing for our lives over his curse, by obeying His will for us. Let us never forget God's law of retribution.

II. Dancing

Someone would readily say, "What is the matter with that preacher talking about dancing?" Well I did say, "I

Believe God." Since I believe God, He sets forth in the Bible examples of dancing the Lord's way and man's way. Dancing as we know is the rhythmic movement of the body, usually done to musical accompaniment. The question I'm sure that is lingering in your mind is, "Can I do the dances of the world and please God?" Not at all, for the Bible says, "Love not the world, neither the things that are in the world. If any man loves the world, the love of the father is not in him." (I John 2:15)

I know in this day that some Christians dance, saying, "It is nothing wrong with it." They will say that the Christian can do the electric slide, but the question we ought to ask is, "Does it bring honor and glory to the Lord?" Dancing in the Bible was done as a way of celebrating joyous occasions as set forth by Exodus 15:20. When Miriam and all the women took timbrels in their hands and danced it was, because the Lord had drowned the Egyptians in the sea.

Also, David danced before the Lord with all his might when the Ark of the Covenant was brought up to Jerusalem from the house of Obed-Edom. (II Samuel 6:14). David's dance was to the Lord and he did it out of gratitude for what the Lord had done for him and the nation Israel.

Dancing in the Bible was not all to the honor and glory of God. Herodias daughter Salome, danced so well before King Herod, that he took an oath to give her whatsoever she would ask. (Matt. 14:6-7). The kind of dancing that Salome did aroused the king so that he was beside himself. You and I both know that whatever kind of dance she performed, it wasn't to the tune of "Amazing Grace."

When I was in the world I tried a few dances to the worldly music, but I knew it wasn't of God. In my day they had the funky Chicken, the twist, push and pull, along with the mash potatoes, not to mention the slow drag. Of all the dances of my day, the slow drag was the favorite of the other brothers and me. Each of us back then, as well as now, do know that slow dragging stirs up the passion in a man and Christians should have no part in it. Young people, you may not have heard of the dances of my day, but it is still wrong for you to be doing the jiggalate and the chicken head; also the skip, C-walk and heel to toe. All of the dancing we ought to be doing should be to the Lord and to Him only. I have seen some of these dance teams doing ungodly dances which bring shame to the Lord's name.

Young folks you should not be dancing to Britney Spears', "Toxic" and Beyonce's "Naughty Girl" because the lyrics to these songs are shocking to the imagination. One of the lyrics of Britney's song is "Tasting the poison paradise from the Devil's cup, and about being high, addicted, ready, and loving it."

Beyonce's lyrics are, "Feeling sexy, feeling nasty, and wanting to take you home with me." Over and over it refers to wanting to be "Your naughty girl, being all yours and coming to party." It says, "I know you want my body" and I love to love you baby."

As Christians you should not contaminate your minds with such trash, but make up in your heart, soul, and mind to give the Lord His due. Britney, Beyonce, Cash Money, nor Fifty Cent can do for you what the Lord can. They are at the top of the charts temporarily, but the Lord Jesus is at the top permanently.

The Bible says, "Wherefore God also hath highly exalted Him, and given Him a name which is above every name: That at the name of Jesus every knee shall bow, of things in Heaven and things in earth, and things under the earth; And that every tongue should confess that Jesus Christ is Lord, to the glory of God the Father." (Philippians 2:9-11).

Today it's not about the entertainers of the world, who are up today and will be down tomorrow, but it should be about our Lord Jesus, which the Bible says, "He died, but three days and three nights later He arose to live and to live forever more."

Conclusion:

I'm glad today that I believe God about things that are in the Bible and how each of us ought to say as never before, "I believe God."

CHAPTER 6

Marriage Part I

Again Christian friends, I come before you with another message on, "I Believe God." These three words, "I Believe God," were spoken by the greatest Christian of all time, the Apostle Paul.

These words that were spoken by him came at a very critical time. The ship he was sailing was being tossed to and fro from a night storm on the Mediterranean Sea. The lives of all that were aboard the vessel were threatened.

The Lord God, seeing and knowing the danger his servant Paul was in dispatched an angel who said, "Fear not Paul; thou must be brought before Caesar: and lo, God hath given thee all them that sail with thee."

The great apostle relayed this message to those aboard by saying, "Wherefore, sirs be of good cheer: for I Believe God, that it shall be even as it was told me."

In essence Paul was saying, "If God said it, I believe it." That is the same mindset I have friends; that if the Lord said it, I also believe it. Showers, what do you believe? I believe the Bible from Genesis 1:1 to Revelation 22:21 rightly divided.

In parts one through five I have shared with you from the Bible on what I believe about many of the issues of our day. We have discussed Alcohol, Gambling, Tattoos, Dancing, Abortion, Hell, Homosexuality and Lesbianism, and other things.

The Bible is plain and clear on each of these things and how we would all do well to believe God on what he has, is, and will continue to say. Let us never doubt what the Lord has said by adding or taking away from it. As the late John R. Rice stated, "Never put a question mark where God has put a period."

I. Marriage

Yes marriage, the one thing the Lord meant for our good, has become evil according to society. Though the Lord is omniscient in knowing all things, I am sure it breaks his heart to see how mankind has turned away from the truth to a lie. The Lord, from the beginning, saw that Adam needed a help mate. "And the Lord caused a deep sleep to fall upon Adam and he slept: and he took one of his ribs, and closed up the flesh instead thereof; and the rib, which the Lord had taken from man, made he a woman, and <u>brought her unto the man.</u>"
"And Adam said this is now bone of my bones, and flesh of my flesh; she shall be called woman, because she was taken out of man. Therefore shall a man leave his father

and his mother, and <u>shall cleave unto his wife</u>: and they shall be one flesh." (Genesis 2:21-25)

The Bible is as clear as can be on who the Lord expects to marry. It is a man who is to marry another woman, not man and man, nor woman and woman. For anyone to go against what the Lord has set forth about marriage is for them to defy God and merely say, "What the Lord meant for Adam and Eve is no longer relevant for this day."

If I love another man and he loves me, or if a woman loves another woman we, they would say, have a right to marry. So do the dogs and cats, but you don't find where God joined them together. The Lord still means, "Whosoever findeth a wife, findeth a good thing" (Proverbs 18:22). He did not say, "Whosoever findeth another man or what woman findeth another woman is a good thing.

It's about the man going after the woman and not vice versa. Ladies, do you desire a husband? If so, wait on him to find you and not you find him. Preacher I have been waiting five or ten years for one to find me. My response to you is, "Keep on waiting." Have you ever thought about the Lord preparing you for what you need? You can't get what the Lord has for you if you are trying Jimmy this month and Joe the next. Settle yourself down and allow God to send you a husband or brothers, if you need a wife the Lord has one for you.

Why was marriage designed? (1) The happiness of man. (2) To increase the species, and (3) To prevent fornication.

I. The Happiness of Man

The Lord, from the beginning, after seeing all had a mate but Adam, decided to give him a helpmeet to make him happy. Brothers and sisters, the Lord wants our marriages to be happy ones and not a long blizzard of unhappiness. Why is there no happiness in your marriage? Did you marry your spouse for the right or wrong reason?

If you married for the right reason the Lord will bless you and cause his face to shine upon you, but if for the wrong reason, you are in it now and the Lord expects you to make the best of it.
No one held a gun on you when you said, "I take this man or woman to be my lawfully wedded one, for better or for worse, for richer or poorer and forsaking all others keeping myself faithfully to my partner till death us do part."

Those words that many of us spoke on that momentous day of marriage will face us again in the judgment when the secrets of all hearts will be disclosed.

Knowing this, it ought to behoove each of us to have the mindset that the Lord wants my marriage to be a happy one and I'm going to give it my all and all. How beautiful it is to see two people in love and happy with the spouse they have chosen. Preacher, how can I be happy in my marriage? By doing all you can to make your spouse happy.

I must say that again, "Do all you can to make your spouse happy." But what if he or she doesn't do anything to make me happy? Just keep on making them happy and the Lord will make you happy. Always remember that your labor is not in vain, when it is done the Lord's way.

Some ways to have a happy marriage (1) Choose a good spouse in the first place. Full of virtue and holy to the Lord. (2) Don't marry until you are sure that you can love entirely. (3) Remember that women are ordinarily affectionate, passionate creatures, and as they love much themselves, so they need love from us. (4) Remember that you are under God's command; and to deny marital love to your wives is to deny a duty which God has urgently imposed on you. Obedience therefore should command your love. (5) Take more notice of the good that is in your spouse than of their faults. Let not the observation of their faults make you forget or overlook their virtues. (6) Don't magnify each other's imperfections until they drive you crazy. Excuse them as far as is right with the Lord. Consider also your own infirmities, and how much your spouse must bear with you. (7) Don't stir up the evil of your spouse, but cause the best in them to be lived out, and lastly, (8) Live before your spouse the life of a prudent, lowly, loving, meek, self-denying, patient, harmless, holy Heavenly Christian.

The Lord, I believe, wants every marriage to be one long honeymoon and it can be if both partners would give it their heart, soul, and mind. So first of all, marriage was designed for the happiness of man.

II. Increase the Species

Why would a man and woman marry if their intentions are not to have children? The Lord from the beginning said, "Be fruitful, and multiply, and replenish the earth, and subdue it."

It has always been God's plan for married couples to have children, not for children to have children. I know in our day it has become acceptable for the unwedded to have children, but that is not God's way.

Those who should be having them are the very ones who are not doing so, and if they happen to get one or two the birth controller is called in. You hear married folk saying, "Children are too expensive," but what they ought to be saying is, "We won't be able to have a fabulous home, we can't have our two or more cars, or we can't have vacations and wear the finest clothing."

Shame on this society when the Lord said, "Lo children are a heritage of the Lord: and the fruit of the womb is his reward. As arrows are in the hand of a mighty man; so are children of the youth. Happy is the man that hath his quiver full of them: they shall not be ashamed, but they shall speak with the enemies in the gate." (Psalms 127:3-5)

The Lord also said, "Thy wife shall be as a fruitful vine by the sides of thine house: Thy children like olive plants round about thy table." (Psalm 128:3)

I am a witness that the Lord's word is true concerning the fruitfulness of a marriage. I dare not be braggadocios, for God knows my heart. My wife's parents had seventeen children, with thirteen still alive and all of them are blessed of the Lord.

My parents had twelve, with seven of us living and the Lord has truly blessed our family. The wife and I have had twelve with ten that are still with us. I could write a book on God's goodness to us because of the children He has given us. One fellow jokingly said, "Yes Showers the Lord said be fruitful and multiply, but He didn't tell you to do it all."

Friends, it's all about the subject matter, "I believe God," whereas others are still thinking that it should be their way and not God's way. Secondly, marriage was designed to increase the species. Finally, it was designed

III. To Prevent Fornication

The Lord instituted marriage for those of us who could not hold it and control it. He never meant for us to try it to see whether or not we liked it. The Lord meant abstinence from the beginning and He still means the same for this day. "Marriage is honorable and the bed undefiled. But whoremongers and adulterers God will judge." (Hebrews 13:4)

The Lord does not have a "safe sex motto" as society says, but a "no sex motto" until marriage. Allow me young and old to say that all sexual aids are a sin and it makes no difference to God what the politicians, parents, The CDC (Center for Disease Control) or anyone else says. The Lord that I believe utters, "To avoid fornication, let every man have his own wife, and let every woman have her own husband." (I Corinthians 7:2)

Someone will readily say, "Didn't you engage in sex before marriage?" Yes, that's why I am warning you not to do so, for I have reaped the consequences of my action. For had I known then what I know now I would have avoided it. We must pay for our mistakes (sins) if we involve ourselves in sex before marriage. AIDS and venereal diseases are the repercussions of our actions.

Conclusion:

I am glad that I believe God on the marriage issue and how I thank the Lord for my thirty one plus years of it. The Bible says, "Therefore shall a man leave his father and mother and shall cleave unto his wife: and they shall be one flesh." (Genesis 2:24)

Let us friends, keep in mind the vows we made to God, our spouses, and those that are assembled. John Ray said, "Wedlock is padlock." that is when we wed another, the Lord expects us to be locked in to each other and Him. Let us in our marriage live so that the Lord can say, "Well done servant, for you have been faithful in your marriage, receive the blessings I have for you."

CHAPTER 7

Marriage Part II

We all are aware by now that the Holy Father expects us to believe him as his servant Paul did in the midst of adversity while sailing on the Mediterranean Sea.

The great apostle did as every born again believer ought to do when the trouble and trials of life are seemingly getting the best of us, our response ought to be, "I believe God."

If ever a time in Christendom, when the Church of the living God ought to believe God, that time is now, I have, with the aid of the Holy Spirit, set forth to you. "I believe God."

What I have shared with you in the previous six messages have not been my own personal opinion about certain issues, but I have imparted to you what the Word of God has said about them.

If you have followed me in this series I have told you that I believe God about homosexual and lesbian issues, how we should dress, tattoos, Hell, dancing, abortion, gambling, women preachers, and marriage. With the leadership of the Holy Spirit, allow me to give you a second message on what I believe about marriage. In our last directive I stated that marriage was designed for the happiness of man, secondly to increase the species and thirdly to prevent fornication.

My question to you is "Did you marry for happiness or for what you could get from your spouse?" If what you could get from your spouse was the reason shame on you and the dreadfulness you must face for doing so. God did not ordain marriage primarily for material gain, though it is important, but God gave us spouses for our spiritual advancement.

If you and I who are married, or those who expect to, do it for any other reason, you have a stolen marriage.

Marriage is so important in the mind of God that it was the first divine institution and was patterned to illustrate God's love for the church.

There is little wonder why the vows we take ought to be in sincerity, as well as in truth. Marriage is sacred and should never be entered into unadvisedly, but advisedly, discreetly, and in the fear of God. Young folks don't elope or run off and get married without some Godly counsel. It is too big of a responsibility to just jump into without being advised.

Let me have your undivided attention and hear some reasons why not to get married. (1) To spite or get back at your parents (2) Fear of being left out! Being left as a bachelor or an old maid (3) Marrying on the rebound – you were hurt in a former love relationship and to ease your hurt you immediately choose another (4) To escape an unhappy home (5) Because you are pregnant, and (6) To show others what you can do.

Some reasons why we should marry: (1) Because you are convinced that it is God's will for you to marry this person (2) Companionship (3) To work together and fulfill your own and your future mate's needs, and (4) To fulfill sexual needs in the way God intends.

The Lord wants us all who are married, and those with the intention of doing so, to know that His plan for marriage is one man, for one woman, for one lifetime.

In essence the Lord meant and still means that marriage should be for as long as the couple lives. Many books, movies, comedians, and magazines make a mockery of marriage, but praise God that he meant if for our good.

By way of outline, I believe God about: (1) The Preparation for Marriage (2) The Plan for Marriage, and (3) The Practice in Marriage

I. **The Preparation For Marriage**

Yes there must be some preparation before you say, "I will take this man or woman to be my lawfully wedded wife or husband."

I'm afraid that most couples get married and spend more time on shopping for wedding gowns, tuxedos, reception halls, and honeymoon sights than they do on preparing for each other.

Get to know your lifetime partner and don't rush into marriage without knowing the positives and negatives of your mate. It is still wise brothers and sisters as the old song says, "Take time to know each other."

In what ways should you prepare? (1) Prepare spiritually (2) Prepare mentally, and (3) prepare financially.

Spiritually, you and your spouse ought to be saved. Don't make the mistake sisters and brothers, thinking once you marry that your partner will become a Christian. If you are a Christian please don't marry an unsaved man or woman because it will be heartaches by the dozens. The Bible emphatically says, "Be ye not unequally yoked together with unbelievers: For what fellowship hath righteousness with unrighteousness and what communion hath light with darkness?" (II Corinthians 6:14).

That's the Lord's word to you, young ladies and gentlemen. Why put yourself at risk by marrying out of the will of God? I would go farther to say to you young folk as well as others, to not even date those whom you know are not in Christ. Remember you are to choose a date that will make you a mate.

Also, along this line of preparation for marriage,

1. Do your best to marry someone of the same faith or belief as you. As nice as a Jehovah Witness may be, young ladies or men, please don't get entangled with one because your life will be in shambles. I know from

experience, because I have relatives that made that mistake. The Bible says, "Can two walk together, except they be agreed?" (Amos 3:3).

2. Prepare mentally for marriage by making sure there is maturity. It is a must. Marriage is not something we should be trying out to see if it works, but have the mindset, "What therefore God hath joined together, let not man put asunder." (Mark 10:9).

3. Prepare financially, that is don't depend on mom and dad to take care of you. It was your choice to marry and in doing so it is your responsibility to carry your own weight. One of the saddest things there is to see are couples that get over their heads in debt preparing for marriage, and after the wedding day, come by mama's house for some red beans and rice. If you are getting married don't spend all your money on one day and forget about life after it. The Bible says, "But if any provide not for his own, and especially for those of

his own house, he hath denied the faith, and worse than an infidel." (I Timothy 5:8)

I remember not long after my wife and I were married, we found out about this couple who was having a hard time of it, and we took them a box of groceries. When we arrived at their home, lo and behold, the husband, a healthy man, was lying down. I told the wife, "Never again."

Have a plan young folks financially. I know a young brother who shared with me on how he and his wife prepared for the finances. He said they would live off of his salary and save hers for future endeavors. There must be financial preparation.

II. **The Plan For Marriage**

The plan we have, or should have, ought to be one of (1) Sharing (2) Surrender (3) Submission, and (4) Showing

The reason God gave Eve to Adam and Adam to Eve was for the purpose of sharing, surrendering, submitting, as well as showing.

1. His plan for sharing commenced when God saw the man alone, so he created the woman so they could share with each other. There should always be sharing between spouses. Believe me, it's a shame before God when two people who are supposed to be one can't share with the other.

2. God's plan for surrender: "Therefore shall a man leave his father and mother and cleave unto his wife: and they shall be one flesh." (Genesis 2:24). Both husband and wife should work as a team. The "me" "my" and "mine" attitudes should become "ours". Not my car, but ours. Not my house, or bank account, but ours. Not my children, but ours. Not mother, father,

grandmother, grandfather, brothers, and sisters- in-law, but ours.

3. God's plan for submission is a dual thing. "Submitting yourselves one to another in the fear of God." (Ephesians 5:21)The husband is to submit to Christ and the wife is to submit to her husband, and the children are to submit to the parents. If each of us would follow our divine role there would be no problems in marriage. But a lot of times man wants the woman to submit to him, when he doesn't submit to Christ. "Wives, submit yourselves unto your own husbands as unto the Lord." (Eph. 5:22) Ladies don't hold back what you are to do. If you do, you defy God. For if you can't submit to your husband, you can't submit to God.

Children, the Bible says, "Obey your parents in the Lord for this is right. Honor thy father and mother, which is the first commandment with promise, that it may be well with thee, and thou mayest live long on the earth." (Ephesians 6:1-3).

The Lord's intention, then as well as now, is for everybody to follow their divine assignment and He made sure of it by recording assignments for the father, mother, and children here in Ephesians 5:21-6:1-4.

4. God's plan for showing is that the husband should love his wife as he loves himself and the wife should respect the husband as is set forth by Ephesians 5:25-32.

III. The Practice in Marriage

There are four things we should practice in marriages to keep them in the will of God (1) Control (2) Cooperation (3) Character (4) Peace

Be sure, husbands and wives, that you practice control. Real love will overlook mistakes and failures. Be sure and read I Corinthians 13. Be sure, husbands and wives, that you practice cooperation. The husband and wife should agree and work together. They should sit down and discuss their differences without anger.

Be sure, husbands and wives, to practice good character toward one another. Don't be sweet as honey to everyone else and be a sour lemon toward your spouse.

Be sure, husbands and wives, to practice peace when there are conflicts. Talk things over. Learn to "give and take." It can't always be your way or her way, but the right way.

Conclusion:

In Marriage, always remember to stay in love and keep working at it. Keep in mind that the "we" comes before the "I". A couple was married for sixty years. When asked the reason for their successful marriage, the wife said, "I fell in love often." She paused, then said, "With the same man." Remember, love, trust, prayer, and understanding will make any marriage a success. Marriage can be Heaven on earth, but you must work at it and don't forget to ask God for help.

CHAPTER 8

Divine Healing

Again, the Lord brings us back to the Acts of the Apostles where He has had us for one year and seven months. The Lord, through the Holy Spirit, has given us much in this book that has built us up in the faith.

Before us, one more time, as has been in our last messages, is the text: "Wherefore sirs, be of good cheer; for I Believe God that it shall be even as it was told me." The Apostle Paul, who spoke these words, was one who had extraordinary faith in the Word of God.

God's word to Paul came in the midst of some unfavorable times. Seemingly, life was about to end for him and the other 275 people that were aboard the ship. But these three words, "I Believe God," awakened him to the fact that God was in control of the elements and there was no need for him to fret or worry.

In this day, my brothers and sisters, with all of the ills of this society that is leading our nation to a moral breakdown, the Holy Father wants us to believe Him. We can't believe the politician, but we can believe God. We can't believe mankind in general, but we can believe God.

These three words, as many of you know, have been our focus in the last seven messages. What the Holy Spirit has guided us to do is to set forth some of the things we believe God about.

I have not given you my opinion on what I believe God about, but what the Bible says. In our past discourses I said that I believe God about Hell, dancing, tattoos, how we should dress, the homosexual and lesbian issue, gambling, women preachers, and marriage.

With the aid of the Holy Spirit, our vocal point will be on Divine Healing.

To those of us who really think about it, how could something as divine healing be so controversial in our day when it has the right name, divine healing?

For when we think of something being divine we automatically think of it as being of God and from God. Though God is divine, all powerful, all knowing, and present everywhere, it would seem like He would be in on all of the so called healings of our day. But those of us that believe God, know unequivocally that everybody will not be healed, no matter who the individual is that says so. Someone would readily say, "Are you minimizing God?" A thousand times no. I am actually maximizing Him, because I believe God can heal and will continue to do so, but at His own pleasure.

I have prayed for the sick and have seen the miraculous power of God heal through me, but I dare not say and give myself a title of being a healer. No matter how much we pray and trust God, there are times when the Lord just doesn't heal.

You and I can pray earnestly for days, months, and years over some sick folk, yet it has to be in the will of God for them to be healed. I hear many praying and using the phrase, "Plead the blood of Jesus" but where did that originate?

The Bible never says, "Plead the blood of Jesus", but it does say, "If we ask anything according to His will, he heareth us." Notice not one time did the Lord tell us to "plead the blood."

These so called faith healers will have us believe that Christians shouldn't get sick, and if you do, it's because we lack the faith for healing. Where is that in the Bible and on what do we base such a thing? How sad it is that these so called faith healers will tell us, "Child, if you have cancer, heart disease, or any other ailments do not claim it." Brothers and sisters, that is a foolish conjecture.

Here I am, a black man, and you say, "you might be black, but don't claim it." Friends, I am what I am no matter how much I disclaim it. If the test says sugar diabetes and you say, "I'm not going to claim it," and begin to eat anything, we will see and know what you have, for either you will pass out or die.

I. What Does the Bible teach About Healing?

Who will we believe about this issue of healing, man or God?

Man, as usual messes up everything that God sets forth for the believer's good. The Bible emphatically teaches that, "Man that is born of a woman, is of a few days and full of trouble. He cometh forth like a flower, and is cut down: he fleeth as a shadow, and continueth not." (Job 14:1-2)

That is to say, because of the sin of Adam and Eve that our bodies are full of trouble. If nothing is troubling your body now, just live a few more years and you will find your eyes getting dim, your teeth starting to decay and dental work must be done. Mr. Arthritis gets in the knees, hands, back, feet and other places. Why is this? Because we are full of trouble. Knowing our troubles that we must face, the Lord stands ready to help us in one way or the other. He can heal us of our sickness, or allow us to endure.

Look how God healed Hezekiah and gave him an additional fifteen years. On the other hand, observe how Job had to endure much pain and sorrow, until God got ready to bring him deliverance.

I know that there are times in all of our lives that we begin to wonder why God allows sickness when it looks like He ought to heal us. Who knows what's best for us, you and me or God? We must know without a doubt that healing is of the Lord and He knows what's best for us, and we should be as the song says. "I put it all in His hands." No matter what the situation or problem, let us put it in the Father's hands.

The Bible also teaches the kinds of healing that various ones received, whether by our Lord or the apostles. Our Lord healed through speaking it or putting his hands on them.

The centurion's son was healed through the faith he had in Jesus. In Matthew 8:13 "Go thy way; and as thou hast believed, so be it done unto you."

Whereas, the man who was blind from his birth received a touch from the Lord for his healing; the Bible says, "Jesus spat on the ground, and made clay of the spittle, and He anointed the eyes of the blind man with the clay and said unto him, go, wash in the pool of Siloam,

(Which is by interpretation Sent.) He went his way therefore and washed, and came seeing.

The woman with the issue of blood also received her healing through a touch, as is set forth in Mark 5: 25-34.

Notification should be made that our Lord didn't partially heal individuals, but He healed them completely. If our healing is not within the confines of God's will, it is in vain. If we are going to do something for the Lord, at least we ought to do it as He did.

II. Why Aren't People Healed Today Like They Were In Biblical Times?

Has God changed? No he has not. "Jesus Christ the same yesterday, today and forever" (Hebrews 13:8) Well, what is wrong then? Is it we don't believe what the

Bible says, "They shall take up serpents; and if they drink any deadly thing, it shall not hurt them; they shall lay hands on the sick, and they shall recover?" (Mark 16:18)

Did that ever happen? Yes it did, for after our Lord's ascension into glory, the apostle's healed many, but since apostolic times there hasn't been much healing. The reason being that the people in Jesus's day, as well as the apostles times; didn't have the complete Word of God as we do in this day. So to authenticate or make people believe in the Lord Jesus Christ, many miracles of healings were performed.

Some of you will readily say, "That's a cop out, but brothers and sisters, the primary healing our Lord wants us to have is a spiritual one, which will draw us much closer to Him than of the physical variety.

III. God's Purpose In Healing

I believe God and each of us ought to believe that, God knows what's best for His children." Those of us with afflictions in our bodies, do they make us pray less or more? I'm sure that most of us have to agree that it is more. There was a time in our Christian lives when prayer wasn't that important, but since afflictions have come on us, we spend much time in prayer. Though it is commendable for us to pray much, let us not wait on the troubles and trials of life to drive us to our knees.

The Bible says, "Men ought to always pray and not faint." (Luke 18:1) that is as believers in Christ, we should always be in a frame of mind to pray.

God's purpose in healing is not all about us, but it's about Him. The Lord will not heal anyone, just to be healing them, but it's for His honor and glory. Every miracle that the Lord performed in healing, was to allow mankind to believe in Him. The four gospels record 35 separate miracles performed by the Lord Jesus Christ.

Of those thirty - five miracles he did, twenty three of them had to do with healing. Each case brought the Lord the honor and glory due His name.

From the healing of the nobleman's son at Cana in Galilee, to the restoring of Malchus ear which Peter cut off, the Lord's healings were worth much.

Why? Because He had a purpose in the healings He performed.

Also, the Lord had and still has a purpose in not healing everyone. There are times God does not heal because we have not repented of certain sins.

If sin is prevalent in our lives we must confess our sins and forsake them. If we do not, the Lord will not bring healing to us. Look how Israel kept trespassing against God and how He would bring certain plagues upon them. But when they repented and cried out to the Lord He forgave them.

The Lord had a purpose in not healing the Apostle Paul. "And lest I should be exalted above measure through the abundance of the revelations, there was given me a thorn in the flesh, the messenger of Satan to buffet me, lest I should be exalted above measure. For this thing I besought the Lord thrice, that it might depart from me. And He said unto me, my grace is sufficient for thee: for my strength is made perfect in weakness. Most gladly therefore will I rather glory in my infirmities, that the power of Christ may rest upon me. Therefore I take pleasure in infirmities, in reproaches, in necessities, in persecution, in distresses for Christ's sake: for when I am weak, then am I strong." (II Corinthians 12: 7-10)

If God has not healed many of us, let us not have a pity party, but say the words of the song, "Rock of Ages":

1. Rock of ages cleft for me, let me hide myself in thee; let the water and the blood, from thy wounded side which flowed, be of sin the double cure, save from wrath and make me pure.
2. Could my tears forever flow, could my zeal no languor know, these for sin could not atone--- Thou must save, and thou alone: In my hand no price I bring, simply to thy cross I cling.

3. While I draw this fleeting breath, when my eyes shall close in death, when I rise to worlds unknown and behold thee on thy throne, Rock of Ages, cleft for me, Let me hide myself in thee.

Conclusion:

Thank God today that He is a divine healer that has never or ever will fail and O how we ought to look to Him daily, and not man for our healing.

Praise the Lord that Jesus Christ came into this world to primarily heal us spiritually and if he sees fit our physical healing will come. He (Jesus) died, was buried, and resurrected for our sins.

CHAPTER 9

Giving, Secret Orders and Spiritual Renewal

These words, "I Believe God", ought to be the motto of every born again believer. For they serve as the basis of whether we are a spiritual Christian or a carnal one. Is it so hard for us to believe God, when we believe everyone else?

All of the heroes of faith in Hebrews 11 were men and women who believed God. Though their faith was tested and tried, each held onto their faith because they believed God.

The man of our text, Paul, could say, "Nevertheless, I am not ashamed, for I know whom I have believed, and am persuaded that He is able to keep that which I have committed unto Him against that day." (II Timothy 1:12)

Oh, friends will you and I believe God? While sailing on the Mediterranean Sea, the man Paul in spite of the tempestuous wind and those who doubted him, he held true to the God of Abraham, Isaac, and Jacob.

The one thing that distinguishes the child of God from the sinner is that one believes God, while the other does not. Though every believer in Christ has a foundational belief, the Lord expects us to have maturity in what we believe.

Paul, without a doubt, believed God as each of us ought, and Oh how in this day and time we should hold fast to Him and believe Him like never before. In our previous messages on this title, "I Believe God," I have with the Spirit's guidance set forth from the Bible what I believe it says about: (1) Women Preachers (2) Homosexuality and Lesbians (3) Dancing (4) Gambling (5) Tattoos (6) Hell (7) Marriage and (8) Divine Healing.

There are three things in today's message that I Believe God about (1) Giving (2) Secret Orders and (3) Spiritual Renewal.

I. Giving

Allow me to say this from the outset that there was a time in my earlier years of marriage and before, that I did not know nor believe God concerning giving. But thanks be to God when I learned better, I started doing better.

In fact now I believe God so much about giving, that I now find myself giving more than ever before. I have found out from believing God that, "The liberal soul shall be made fat." (Proverbs 11:25)

I really want to be a super heavy weight in my giving, for I believe the song says, "The more you give the more He gives to you, just keep on giving because it's really true, that you can't beat God's giving, no matter how you try."

In reality, brothers and sisters, I am playing catch up; and though I can't pay God back for all He has given me, I certainly ought to be trying.

Someone said, and I quote, "You are never more like God, than when you give." Let each of us grasp that saying and begin this day doing so.

"How should I give preacher?" The commencement or starting point, in giving is the tithe or ten percent of your earnings. "But preacher, that is too much." Do you believe God? If so, you will immediately begin to implement God's plan for giving.

Once you start with the tithe, or ten percent, there goes along with it an offering. "How much of an offering?" Allow God to dictate that to you and I believe God will tell each of us, "Don't you think it's time for you to graduate from a $1.00?" How long have you been giving God one dollar?

If some of us would be honest, we have been giving one dollar for ten years or more. There is nothing on the market that's still a dollar after ten years. Brothers and sisters, don't you think that God deserves a raise? We will readily ask our employers for a raise, well the Lord this day is asking for one.

Concerning our giving, hear these scriptures, "Upon the first day of the week let every one of you lay by him in store, as God hath prospered him, that there be no gatherings when I come." (I Corinthians 16:2) "But this I say, He which soweth sparingly shall reap also sparingly; and he which soweth bountifully shall reap also bountifully, every man according as he purposeth in his heart, so let him give; not grudgingly, or of necessity: for God loveth a cheerful giver." (II Corinthians 9: 6-7)

"It is more blessed to give than to receive." (Acts 20:35b) "Bring ye all the tithe into the store house, that there may be meat in mine house and prove me now here with, saith the Lord of hosts, if I will not open to you the windows of Heaven, and pour you out a blessing, that there shall not be room enough to receive it. And I will rebuke the devourer for your sakes, and he shall not destroy the fruits of your ground; neither shall your vine cast her fruits before the time in the field, saith the Lord of hosts." (Malachi 3:10-11)

To the few that say that tithing is under the law, remember this saying (tithing commenced with Abraham, continued with Jacob, commanded by Malachi and commended by the Lord Jesus.)

I know that the Lord primarily promised this to the nation Israel, but I believe God wants us to make application of it to ourselves.

Jesus said, "Give and it shall be given unto you; good measure, pressed down, and shaken together, and running over, shall men give into your bosom. For with the same measure that ye mete withal it shall be measured to you again." (Luke 6:38).

The author is unknown that said, "Give according to your income, lest God make your income according to your giving."

I believe God when it comes to the so called:

II. Secret Orders

Just what is this preacher talking about when he says, "Secret Orders"? I am referring to the sororities and fraternities, along with the Masons and Eastern Stars. The question that comes to mind is "Why, and for what reason are these societies called secret orders?" "If they are all that good for you and I to join, why can't the prospects be told what to expect, and the inside scoop of them?"

The members will tell you that they are sworn to secrecy and cannot reveal to outsiders what goes on inside. How strange is this when I have seen great numbers of professing Christians as members of these secret orders?

All Christians should know that there should be nothing secret about the Christian life. The Lord Jesus did not have any secrets, why should men and women of these societies?

Jesus said, "I spake openly to the world; I even taught in the synagogue; and in the temple, whither the Jews always resort; and in secret have I said nothing." (John 18:20)

Now, brothers and sisters, if the Lord Jesus did not have secrets, where did men and women get the idea that they can have some? All sincere Christians should leave, or not have any part, in these so called secret orders.

Yes, I have been approached by some members to become a part of the orders, but after consultation with an old preacher, he said, "Son, you don't need to be a part of such a thing."

The Lord says to us as believers, "Be ye not unequally yoked together with unbelievers; for what fellowship hath righteousness with unrighteousness? And what communion hath light with darkness?" (II Corinthians 6:4)

Anyone holding fast to secrets of which cannot bring the Lord honor and glory, ought to be banished by the believers in Christ.

I have seen, and know of many of our young folks who enroll in college and are solicited to become members of certain fraternities and sororities. Believe me that you can be successful without doing so. The leaders of these orders will have you believe that to get at the top of the ladder: you ought to unite with them. What you ought to tell them is "I Believe God" and He has told me, "Trust in the Lord with all your heart; and lean not unto your own understanding. In all your ways acknowledge Him, and he shall direct my paths." (Proverbs 3:5-6)

There is a book that I recommend to those who are in secret orders, and it is: "Lodges Examined by the Bible," whose author is John R. Rice. So, friends today, I believe God when it comes to secret orders.

Lastly, I believe God that we need:

III. National Renewal

Every great nation of days past needed a national renewal, but instead of them being renewed by the power of the Most High God, they succumb to doing things their way, which brought them utter destruction. Of all the places which were warned to have a renewal or to be revived, only one in scripture believed God and escaped His wrath. The city of Nineveh, as the Bible records, repented of their wickedness and was saved from degradation because they heard and believed the preaching of Jonah.

His message was "Yet forty days and Nineveh shall be overthrown" (Jonah 3:4). Those men and women turned from their evil ways to the Lord which brought them deliverance. Though Ninevah was spared because she repented, she fell back into sin and God had to punish her.

Oh, America, the Lord is calling for national repentance. We were established upon the principles of God's word, but that same word we were founded upon has become mockery today.

In our previous messages on, "I Believe God," you have heard how low we have fallen. The word, which at one time was honored, still says:" Jesus Christ, the same yesterday, today and forever more." (Hebrews 13:8)

He has not changed, but we have through the acceptance of homosexuals and lesbians, alcohol, gambling, adultery, and many other ills of society. What the Lord is saying to us is, "If my people which are called by my name, shall humble themselves, and pray, and seek my face and turn from their wicked ways; then will I hear from Heaven, and will forgive their sin, and will heal their land." (II Chronicles 7:14) Brothers and sisters, that is the Lord's prescription for any nation, as well as any individual, to have national renewal. As the church of the Living God, it is incumbent upon us to get revived for our own survival.

This passage, in II Chronicles 7:14, is for us to awaken out of our sleep, see our moral decline, and do something about it. Let us not say what others need without first beholding ourselves and seeing ourselves first.

What can we do, or better yet, what can I do to bring about renewal? (1) We can develop the desire to know Jesus Christ better. We should have what Dr. George Sweeting calls, "A holy dissatisfaction." (2) We should pray for a change in our lives, that is throwing our entire life into the will of God. (3) We must commit ourselves to obedience to the Great Commission. (4) Our repentance must be complete. "Godly sorrow worketh repentance to salvation not to be repented of." (II Corinthians 7:10) When we cry out: "Create in me clean heart," let us work at keeping it that way. (5) We need to make the crooked straight, that is pay those whom you owe. Be like Zacchaeus who said, "If I have taken anything by false accusation, I restore him fourfold" (Luke 19:8). The Bible says, "Owe no man anything" (Romans 13:8). (6) Develop a seriousness of purpose or don't let anything detour you, but work for the Lord with heart, soul, and mind.

Finally, let us major in the major things of life and aim to please Him which has brought us out of darkness into His marvelous light.

Let us, in the conclusion of our series, "I Believe God" have the mindset that it's not about me, but it's all about Him.

For if I believe Him (Jesus), who says nothing shall be impossible for those who believe in Him, for we should be leaning on the everlasting arms. Oh, in this day and hour, for those of us that will believe God, hear the Lord again through this great preacher: "Wherefore sirs be of good cheer; for I believe God, that it shall be even as it was told me." (Acts 27:25)

Let each of us say, "If Paul could believe God in the midst of his storm, so will I when the crisis of life arrives in mine."

Chapter 10

King James Version, Capital Punishment, The Christian Life

These three words, "I Believe God" stand as the foundation of whether we will be spiritual, natural or carnal. For one to be spiritual in the eyes of the Lord, he or she must believe everything the Lord has, is, and will continue to say in the Holy Scriptures.

The natural person doesn't believe anything that God says because his very nature is an enemy of the true God. The carnal individual is one that believes God for salvation, but has allowed the Devil, the flesh, and the world to overtake him or her.

Thanks be to the Father, Son, and Holy Spirit that the believers of old remained faithful in believing God in spite of the three enemies mentioned above. Those that remained dedicated to the Lord were of the spiritual variety and of the three, will be the only one which the Lord will say, "Well done good and faithful servant too."

The eleventh chapter of Hebrews sets forth to us those of the spiritual class which absolutely could say, "I Believe God." Is that you and I today that can say, "Lord if Enoch, Abel, Noah, Abraham, and others could believe you, so will I?

I'm sure the Apostle Paul of our text is one that said, "I Believe God", for time after time he demonstrated his belief by enduring hardness as a good soldier of Jesus Christ.

In this great text before us, he could have done like others before and now, but he knew that all things were possible unto those who took God at His word.

Friends, for you and I to say, "I Believe God", we must take Him at His word. If there is one thing the Lord expects of His children, it is for us to believe Him. There are two avenues we can take toward God. We can believe everything about Him or doubt all things about Him. As Alfred Korzylski says, "Both ways save us from thinking." In light of that statement, let us thunder out loud and clear, "I Believe God"

It is my prayer that many of us that have heard our previous messages on "I Believe God" that you would accept and believe what he says about women preachers, homosexuality and lesbians, alcohol, gambling, tattoos, dancing, Hell, marriage, divine healing, the secret orders of our day, giving, and the call for spiritual renewal.

This message today, which will be our tenth in this series on "I Believe God," will focus on (1) KJV (2) Capital Punishment and (3) The Christian life

I. The Bible

Friends, Do you believe that the Lord is smiling or frowning with all the different Translations of the Bible? Many theologians as well as parishioners are getting away from the Authorized Version of the King James Bible.

The K. J. V. is becoming obsolete in many of our pulpits and to justify it, some are saying that King James was a homosexual. What they don't tell you is, the man that started this was an officer in the royal household, by the name of Sir Anthony Welden. He and King James had a falling out, and the King fired him. Weldon swore he would get revenge and waited twenty- five years after the King died before he made his accusation.

Disgruntled courtiers and political opponents picked up the allegations against King James and began to use innuendos to hurt his reputation. Some historians began to repeat these attacks against the King without investigation and began to report them as historical facts.

In our day, homosexual activists have been determined to claim King James as one of their own, as well as some biblical characters.

Those who would speak against King James ought to read what some of his contemporaries had to say about him. In 1602, Sir Henry Wotton said, "Among his good qualities none shine more brightly than the chasteness of his life." Bishop Godfrey Goodman wrote, "The king himself was a very chaste man." Others of which I could name esteem the character of the King. King James was married and had 9 siblings.

If the king was a homosexual as the critics would say, why would he in his book, "Basilicon Doron" say, "There are some horrible crimes that ye (to his son) are bound in conscience never to forgive: such as witchcraft, willful murder, incest, and sodomy (homosexual activity)"?

In July of 1610, King James was asked to pardon a number of criminals. He did pardon several on the list but refused to pardon those convicted of sodomy. The king repeatedly referred to homosexuality as the "horrible crime!"

So, brothers and sisters, don't shy away from the KJV because of false statements about the one who had the Bible translated into the English language. Let each of us get back to the study and public reading of the Authorized King James Version.

Many of our modern translations such as the NIV, NKJV, RSV, NASB, LB, and The Women's Devotional Bible should be read in private, but not publicly. In fact a lot of these translations either add to the Word of God, or take away from it. The two most popular versions used in our day are the NKJV and the NIV. There is a book written by Rev. Charles Salliby that we would do well to read because it sets forth many omissions of the scriptures. The title of the book is, "If The Foundations Be Destroyed."

In the NIV the title "Christ" has been removed forty-five times, the name "Jesus" removed forty-six times, and the title "Lord" thirty- one times. The Lord, brothers and sisters, would have us say, "I Believe God" in giving us the KJV Bible.

II. Capital Punishment

There has been much debate about this issue simply because mankind wants to put his ideas and thoughts where the Lord is clear. There are no clouds or fog in what the Lord has said in His argument for capital punishment.

To many of you that will listen to the public view of this matter you ought to listen to the Lord and what He says about the issue of capital punishment. When I was a young minister, just starting in the ministry, I can remember an alliance of preachers that assembled for debate on this issue. I along with an aged pastor believed what the Bible said, while the others gave their opinions.

Though I was probably the youngest preacher in the assembly, I still believed that God is for capital punishment as the Bible sets forth. I was black balled by some, but I held onto my convictions, because I believed God.

How can you, a Pastor / Teacher, believe in such a thing? Because God commands it. According to Genesis 9:6, capital punishment is based upon a belief in the sanctity of life. It says, "Whosoever shed man's blood, by man his blood shall be shed, for in the image of God, he made man."

There are two reasons for God making this known to Noah and his sons. (1) To deter one from taking another man's life, and (2) because man is made in the image of God. Who are you and I to take it upon ourselves to kill? Can we replace what God has created and made? A thousand times no, so let us then think hard and long about taking another person's life.

Capital punishment someone would argue is against God's law of, "Thou shalt not kill", but if you would study the scripture, the Lord is saying, "Thou shalt not commit murder." What we must know is: it is not for me to kill another because they have killed one of my own, but the Lord ordained government to take care of the perpetrator.

That's why the Lord says in Romans 13:1-4, "Let every soul be subject unto the higher powers. For there is no power but of God: the powers that be are ordained of God. Whosoever therefore resisteth the power resisteth the ordinance of God: and they that resist shall receive to themselves damnation. For rulers are not a terror to good works, but to the evil. Wilt thou then not be afraid of the power? Do that which is good, and thou shalt have praise of the same, for he is the minister of thee for good. But if thou do that which is evil, be afraid; for he beareth not the sword in vain; for he is the minister of God, a revenger to execute wrath upon him that doeth evil."

When the state or government executes one, or as some that are given lethal injection, they are merely following God's order. Someone will say, "but it won't be a dent in crime." If it was carried out God's way, I guarantee you it will. In Numbers 15:32-37, a man was found gathering up sticks on the Sabbath as God had commanded it not to be done. They put the brother in ward, or we would say in jail until Moses inquired of God what to do. God told Moses to have him stoned with stones till he dies. You don't read where anyone else picked up sticks against the Lord's will.

I know that there are many of you who are against capital punishment because of what you have heard politicians and religious leaders say, but I would admonish you to believe God and not man.

III. The Christian Life

Brothers and sisters, do you know anything better than being a Christian? If so, please tell me so I can be a part of it. I am having the best time of my life in being a Christian. To the young folks, being a Christian is not boring, but it's excitement.

I can say with Nehemiah, "The joy of the Lord is my strength." (Nehemiah 8:10). Not the fancy clothes, cars, or homes of my day, but the joy of the Lord is my strength.

I believe God that the Christian life has a better pay day than the sinner who lives his life in harmony with the Devil and his demons. The Christian's pay day will result in crowns for our crosses, whereas the sinner will have the lake of fire and brimstone for his reward.

The Christian life has its beginning in Christ with no end in sight, whereas the sinner will have eternity to be with the Devil who fooled you into thinking that you had time to become a Christian.

An unknown author wrote:

"What can the world offer you without Jesus? To be without Jesus is Hell most grievous, to be with Jesus is to know the sweetness of Heaven. If Jesus is with you, no enemy can harm you. Whoever finds Jesus, finds a rich treasure, and a good above every good. He who loses Jesus loses much indeed, and more than the whole world. Poorest of all is he who lives without Jesus, and richest of all is he who stands in favor with Jesus."

"The blessedness of the Christian life gives us the Kingdom of Heaven, though we are poor in spirit. Though we mourn, yet we shall be comforted. Our meekness will inherit the earth. Our hungering and thirsting after righteousness will fill us."

"Our being merciful will enable us to obtain mercy. Our pure hearts will enable us to see God. Our being peacemakers will enable us to be called the children of God. Our persecution for righteousness sake gives us the Kingdom of Heaven."

Chapter 11

Civil Government and Christian Education

Here again the Lord has brought us together, one more time to hear another message on the words uttered by the Apostle Paul as he encountered a mighty storm on the Mediterranean Sea.

Those three words," I Believe God" will never be forgotten by you the members of the Body of Christ.

If all of the members of the Body of Christ would only believe God, think of the difference we could make in society. Why do we make it so hard to believe God?

All He wants is for us to believe Him. I know that many of us believe God for salvation, but what else do we believe God for?

How sad it will be for us as Christians to stand at the Judgment Seat of Christ where the secrets of all hearts will be disclosed, and the Lord Jesus will say "You did not add anything to the Salvation I imparted to you." Why could you not believe me for anything else? Oh, the detrimental effect of us as Christians to not believe God. It will result in us being ashamed in Heaven because we shamed Him by not believing Him on earth.

The man of our text, the Apostle Paul, without a doubt was one that believed God in spite of his circumstances. Can any of us stand today and say, "For I am persuaded that neither death, nor life, nor angels, nor principalities, nor powers, nor things present, nor things to come nor height, nor depth, nor any other creature, shall be able to separate us from the love of God which is in Christ Jesus, our Lord." (Romans 8:38-39)?

How could Paul utter such words without being fearful? Because he believed God. From his salvation experience on the Damascus Road until Nero chopped off his head, the great apostle believed God. We can't believe

God about some things without believing him about all things.

In our previous ten messages on "I believe God" we have studied what the Bible teaches about Hell, tattoos, dancing, women preachers, marriage, divine healing, homosexuality and lesbianism, gambling, giving, the secret order of our day, the Christian life, and what we believe about the authorized King James version of the Bible.

In this, our eleventh message on "I believe God", let us see what the Bible says about (1) Civil Government, (2) Christian Education

1. Civil Government

    Civil government did not get its start when the Declaration of Independence was signed on July 4, 1776. No brothers and sisters, the Lord God instituted it.

    Everything that the Lord God ever implemented was for the betterment of mankind. Though the Lord meant civil government for our good, we know it has been abused and misused by man.

Taxation began as a compulsory fee or financial contribution for the maintenance of government. Taxes may have originated with the custom of giving presents for protection from harm (Genesis 32:13-21; 33:10; 43:11). When Joseph revealed to the Pharaoh in Egypt that there would be seven years of famine after seven years of abundance, Pharaoh put him in charge of raising revenue.

During the time of famine, as well as plenty, he collected a 20 percent tax to store up food and then to buy land for Pharaoh (Genesis 47: 20-26).

During the time of the Exodus, the Lord had Moses to ask for voluntary revenue for the construction of the tabernacle (Exodus 25:2; 35:5, 21) The Mosaic Law prescribed that every male over the age of 20 was to give half a shekel for the service of the tabernacle

(Exodus 30:11-16). With the establishment of the United Kingdom under David and Solomon several avenues of taxation were established: a 10 percent tax on the produce of land and livestock (I Samuel 8: 15, 17).

The oppressive taxation by Solomon was one of the causes of the split of the Kingdom after his death (I Kings 12:4). Taxation continued throughout the Old Testament and continued in the New. The Lord Jesus subjected Himself to the paying of taxes.

In St. Matthew 17: 24-27 those that received tribute money came to Peter and said, "Doth not your master pay tribute?" Jesus told Peter, "Go thou to the sea, and cast a hook, and take up the fish that first cometh up. And when thou hast opened its mouth, thou shalt find a piece of money; then take, and give unto them for me and thee."

By divine providence there went out a decree from Caesar Augustus that all the world should be taxed. With Joseph being from Bethlehem he took Mary and they went to pay their taxes. While there, as we know, the Savior of the world was born.

Not only does civil government have the authority to collect taxes, but also the God whom I believe set it up to mete out punishment to those who don't obey its laws. As Christians, we have a divine obligation to subject ourselves to civil government as long as it does not come into conflict with the Lord and our obedience to Him. The Bible sets forth in Romans 13:1-7 how we are to be towards government.

Though civil government has its flaws, the Lord will hold it accountable for not doing as it should. Capital punishment should be done fairly and without respect of persons. The Lord initiated it for two reasons. One is to deter man from taking another man's life. Secondly, is because man is made in the image of God.

When a person takes it upon himself to kill another, the God whom I believe says, "That man shall be killed." In Genesis 9:6 "Whoso sheddeth man's blood, by man shall his blood be shed: for in the image of God made he man.

"That is to say that the system which God has ordained must mete out the punishment.

If civil government was as aggressive in carrying out punishment for murderers as they are about collecting taxes, our murder rate and crime in general will be down. But because we don't believe God in doing things as he commanded, our society is suffering from it.

To those who don't believe that God's way is the best way if we would carry it out his way, ought to read

Numbers 14:32-37. A man was found gathering up sticks on the Sabbath as God had commanded for it not to be done. Because of this man's disobedience God told Moses to have him stoned with stones till he die. Did that deter anyone else from gathering sticks on the day it wasn't to be done? Yes it did, and so would the same be done in this day if only the government believed God. I believe God that civil government is of and by him.

II. THE CHRISTIAN'S EDUCATION

Much is said in our day, as well as in days past, about the importance of education. But most of our energy and time is spent on secular education.

I dare not minimize the significance of the secular variety, for it is needed. James Brown, in the 60's, sang a song which said, "Without an education you might as well be dead."

In his song he was emphasizing to our young people to go to school and learn, so they can be productive in society. Mr. Brown was singing of a secular education which is fine and dandy, but the God whom I believe, wants them to be educated spiritually. For the Israelites, the goal of education was to prepare people to know God and to live peaceably with one another. The emphasis ought not be the three R's, but the true God. Children were educated in the home by the parents. However, by New Testament times, schools had been established to assist parents in the teaching of their children.

God gave the responsibility of teaching to parents (Deuteronomy 11:19) "And you shall teach them to your children, speaking of them when thou sittest in thine house, and when thou walkest by the way, when thou liest down, and when thou risest up."

To be a parent meant to teach. Both parents were involved in the child's education; however the father was responsible to see that his children were properly educated (Proverbs 1:8-9). A young son stayed with his mother when the father went to the fields to work. Therefore, a boy's first significant instruction came from his mother (Proverb 31:1-9) a daughter also stayed with her mother and continued under her instruction. In the close-knit family structure of that day, as parents became grandparents they also became involved in teaching their grandchildren (Deuteronomy 4:9; II Timothy 1:5; 3:14-15). The instruction of children continued until death.

Friends today, do we believe God? If so, we must get back to teaching our children spiritual things that will enable them to grow up and be responsible parents themselves.

The Lord expects us who believe in Him to have a good Christian education. There is no need for any child of God to be ignorant about spiritual things. The Lord that called us and saved us is spiritual, so should we be.

People in the secular world can get their degrees, why can't we strive to get them in Christendom? The Lord still means for us his children to "Study to shew thyself approved unto God, a workman that needeth not to be ashamed, rightly dividing the word of truth." (II Timothy 2:15)

There is no time for us to cease our study of the Word of God, for I believe that it should be till death us do part. Though the apostle Paul was facing death, yet in his waning moments he instructed Timothy to come before winter, and at his coming bring the books, but especially the parchments!

As Christians, we should not let a day go by without us reading and meditating on the Word of God. Jesus said, "Man shall not live by bread alone, but by every word that proceeded out of mouth of God" (Matthew 4:4).

"Thy Word of God have I hid in mine heart that I might not sin against thee" (Psalm 119:11).

"Thy word is a lamp unto my feet, and a light unto my path" (Psalm 119:105).

Each of us today ought to say, "Educate me Lord; Educate me till I want no more."

Oh how the Lord longs to feed us with that bread of which we will never hunger anymore. No Christian should be without education.

I thank God for the Christian education he has given me and I am striving to get more. From 1988-1998, the Lord took me from an associate's degree to a Doctorate of

Theology, but it's not over for me. I must still apply myself to a study of the Word of God and so should you.

CONCLUSION:

Let us today, say that," I believe God" on what he says about Civil Government of which he has ordained. Along with believing God about Civil Government, I also believe him about Christian Education, which can enable me to grow in grace and in the knowledge of our Lord Jesus Christ.

In acquiring this education as a Christian, "I will find out that God's word upholds (Psalm 119:116), it orders steps (Psalm 119:133), it produces joy (Psalm 119:162), it strengthens (Psalm 119:28); I John 2:14, it gives hope (Psalm 119:74,81), it gives light (Psalm 119:105,130), it gives understanding Psalm (119:169), it shows God's will (Isaiah 55:11), it builds up (Acts 20:32), it produces fruit (John 15:7) , it convicts of sin (Hebrew 4:12), it convicts the soul (James 1:18), 1 Peter 1:23, it cleanses the conscience (John 15:3), it consecrates life (John 17:17), it correct the wrong (II Timothy 3:16), it confirms the right (John 8:31), it comforts the heart (Psalm 119:50,54)." DL Wilmington

The Lord God inspired Paul Rader to write this song, "Only Believe"

"Fear not, little flock, from the cross to the throne, From death into life He went for his own; all power in earth, all power above, is given to Him for the flock of His love."

Chorus: "Only believe, only believe; all things are possible, only believe."

Bibliography

The New Encyclopedia of Christian Quotations
   Mark Water

Encyclopedia of Illustrations—Paul Lee Tan

Practical Sermon Outlines---Croft M. Pentz

6, 000 Sermon Illustrations – Elon Foster

That Manuscript from outer Space D.L. Wilmington

Why The Devil Desires To Damn You—Oliver B. Greene

www.ingramcontent.com/pod-product-compliance
Lightning Source LLC
Chambersburg PA
CBHW051836090426
42736CB00011B/1837